DECISIONS, AGENCY, AND ADVISING

DECISIONS, AGENCY, AND ADVISING

Key Issues in the Placement of Multilingual Writers into First-Year Composition Courses

TANITA SAENKHUM

UTAH STATE UNIVERSITY PRESS
Logan

© 2016 by the University Press of Colorado

Published by Utah State University Press
An imprint of University Press of Colorado
5589 Arapahoe Avenue, Suite 206C
Boulder, Colorado 80303

 The University Press of Colorado is a proud member of
The Association of American University Presses.

The University Press of Colorado is a cooperative publishing enterprise supported, in part, by Adams State University, Colorado State University, Fort Lewis College, Metropolitan State University of Denver, Regis University, University of Colorado, University of Northern Colorado, Utah State University, and Western State Colorado University.

The paper used in this publication meets the minimum requirements of the American National Standard for Information Sciences—Permanence of Paper for Printed Library Materials. ANSI Z39.48–1992

ISBN: 978-1-60732-540-6 (paperback)
ISBN: 978-1-60732-548-2 (ebook)

Library of Congress Cataloging-in-Publication Data

Names: Saenkhum, Tanita, 1976– author.
Title: Decisions, agency, and advising : key issues in the placement of multilingual writers into first-year composition courses / Tanita Saenkhum.
Description: Logan : Utah State University Press, [2016] | Includes bibliographical references.
Identifiers: LCCN 2016023037 | ISBN 9781607325406 (pbk.) | ISBN 9781607325482 (ebook)
Subjects: LCSH: Counseling in higher education. | English language—Rhetoric—Study and teaching (Higher)—Foreign speakers. | Multilingual persons—Education (Higher) | English language—Rhetoric—Evaluation.
Classification: LCC LB2343 .S24 2016 | DDC 808/.0420711—dc23
LC record available at https://lccn.loc.gov/2016023037

Cover illustration © BNMK0819/Shutterstock.

For Afia, Joel, Jonas, Pascal, Jasim,
Ting, Chan, Mei, Askar, Marco, Ana,
and all my multilingual student writers

To my father and mother, who have
inspired me to be an educator

CONTENTS

PREFACE

I have been researching issues related to the placement of multilingual writers—including international visa students and US residents or citizens who are non-native users of English—into college composition courses for six years, and the study reported in this book is one of my research outcomes. Particularly, this book grew out of a placement case of Juan (pseudonym), a student who was placed into English 101 (First-Year Composition) when he first entered a US university (see details in chapter 1). Juan decided to switch to my multilingual composition section in the second semester of his college career. At that time, as a graduate teaching assistant, I did not fully understand how placement worked and kept wondering how Juan ended up taking a mainstream composition course in the first place and why he wanted to take my second language writing (L2) class.

With those questions in mind, I started out asking a very simple yet critical question: how do multilingual writers like Juan make decisions about placement into a mainstream or multilingual composition course? From there, I followed 11 multilingual students from various language backgrounds who made their placement decisions about first-year writing courses over the course of one academic year in one of the country's biggest writing programs. Their candid, thorough, and honest first-year composition placement experiences featured in this book did answer my question, giving me a better and greater understanding of multilingual students' placement decision-making process. Their placement stories also allowed me to investigate how they exercised *agency* in their placement decisions and, in turn, to develop my theory of agency. As a researcher and writing program administrator (WPA), I always find ways to put theory into practice. To be more specific, this book explores how student agency can inform the overall programmatic placement of multilingual students in college composition programs. It also discusses how the studied writing program has used what they have learned about that decision-making process to improve the placement practices for multilingual students and, in particular, how they advise students about placement. At my own institution, I have constantly applied what I have learned from my own research to cope with some placement-related issues.

This book is written for a wide range of audiences, including:

- WPAs who continue to determine appropriate placement practices that can meet the needs of multilingual writers
- Scholars/researchers investigating second language writing and first-year composition placement
- Academic advisors who are working toward the success of multilingual students in order to support their institutions' rapid internationalization
- University-level administrators involved with advising and international programs
- Graduate students interested in second language writing and writing program administration for multilingual writers
- Graduate students in rhetoric and composition programs who wish to learn more about the placement of multilingual writers in college composition programs
- Writing teachers who are currently or will be working with multilingual writers

ACKNOWLEDGMENTS

I am thankful for having great people around me; their help and support has made this book possible. First and foremost, my deepest gratitude goes to the eleven multilingual writers who allowed me to follow them for the entire academic year to learn about their first-year composition placement experiences. And we became friends. My sincere thanks also go to the four academic advisors, five writing teachers, and two WPAs for their willingness to share insightful perspectives on the placement of multilingual students into college composition courses, which makes this book richer.

I owe special thanks to my lifetime (he said I have his permission) mentor Paul Kei Matsuda for his tremendous help with this project, especially when I was in the process of theorizing agency. His work on second language writing (L2) has inspired me as a researcher and WPA. I would like to extend my thanks to Anthony Welch, my faculty mentor at the University of Tennessee, Knoxville for his thorough and constructive comments on an early draft of my first two chapters; likewise to my wonderful L2 writing folks Todd Ruecker and Deborah Crusan for their insightful commentary. And thank you Todd and Jay Jordan for sharing with me their book proposals. My thanks also go to Keith Miller of Arizona State for his feedback on my book proposal and two sample chapters. I thank Matthew Hammill for his help with testing the reliability of my interview coding schemes.

I am grateful for all the different kinds of support and help I have received from the Department of English at UT Knoxville: first, words of encouragement and guidance from my former

department head, Stan Garner, and current department head,
Allen Dunn; my writing buddy and dear friend and colleague,
Lisa King, for writing together once a week for three years and
for listening to what I have to say about writing this book; my
RWL friends and colleagues: Janet Atwill and Kirsten Benson
for their helpful feedback on my book proposal; and Jeff Ringer
for sharing with me his book proposal and of course words
of encouragement like "You can do it, Tanita." I thank all my
English colleagues for their support and encouragement and
our administrative staff (Judith Welch, Donna Bodenheimer,
and all) for their enormous help with everything. With the support from the Department's 2013 and 2014 Summer Hodges
Research Grants and research leave in Spring 2015, I was able
to complete this book. The Office of Research and Engagement
and the Humanities Center at the University of Tennessee
awarded a publication subvention to this book. I thank Joe
Wilson for helping me proofread the typeset pages. This project was also supported in part by the 2010–2011 Conference on
College Composition and Communication Research Initiative.
At Arizona State, where my research took place, I am thankful
for the help and support from Shirley Rose, Mark James, and
Demetria Baker.

At University Press of Colorado/Utah State University Press,
I am thankful to Michael Spooner, associate director, for his
support for my book along the way. It has been a great plea-
sure to work with you, Michael. Thanks for always keeping me
informed of all the processes of book publication. I would like
to thank two reviewers whose comments helped strengthen my
book. I also thank Laura Furney, Anya Hawke, Allie Madden,
Daniel Pratt, Darrin Pratt, and Beth Svinarich for their help
with the production of this book. I am glad to have the opportunity to work with this amazing team.

I have a number of friends near and far who always believe in
me, and I would like to thank them: Soo Hyon Kim, Chatwara
Duran, and Aimy Hemmawun Khunmanee.

Finally and importantly, I thank my family—father, mother,
younger brother and sister—for their immense support and

absolute love. They are the BEST. Every conversation on long distant calls, Skype, and FaceTime always encouraged me to do my best and to finish this book. Special thanks go to my brother who helped design a random strategy for recruiting the multilingual student participants.

DECISIONS, AGENCY, AND ADVISING

1

INTRODUCTION
This Is Where It Begins

Juan:	Teacher, I wanted to let you know that I took English 101 last semester.
Tanita:	Hmm . . . Why are you in my class, instead of English 102?
Juan:	My English 101 teacher told me that English 108 would be better for me.
Tanita:	Sounds good to me.

It was a brief conversation between my student and me after our first class meeting ended; it was also the first time I learned about *placement*. Juan was originally from Puerto Rico, and he took my English 108 (a second-semester first-year writing course designed for students whose first or strongest language is not English) in Fall 2009 at Arizona State University (ASU).[1]

To be honest, as a graduate teaching assistant, I did not know how to respond to the student at that moment, so I just said, "sounds good to me," as a way to acknowledge his reply to my question. After Juan left, I asked myself many questions: how did Juan end up in a mainstream composition course in the first place? Why did he decide to take English 101? What went into his placement decision process? Juan's (mis?) placement case, together with a quest for answers to my own questions, was the jumping-off point for my research into the placement of multilingual writers[2] into college composition courses and also the origin of this book. Multilingual writers mentioned in this book include international visa students and US residents or citizens who are non-native English speaking students. In the remainder of this book, when I refer to the two groups of these

DOI: 10.7330/9781607325482.c001

multilingual writers, I will use "international multilingual" and "resident multilingual."

Five years later, I have experienced similar placement cases. As the director of English as a second language (ESL) at my current institution, I have always received email inquiries from students like the one below:

> My name is Vincent Prezer. I am currently a sophomore. I need assistance with my writing since English is my second language. I spoke with the English Department and I was told to speak to you to see what courses I should take to improve my writing.

I met with Vincent, a US citizen student, to discuss his placement, and I learned that he previously took English 101. I informed the student what options he had for a second-semester first-year writing course, explaining to him differences and similarities between English 102 and English 132, an equivalent of 102 specifically designed for multilingual students. I did not tell the student what course he should take but let him decide based on information he received from me. Two weeks later, the student emailed me, letting me know that he decided to take English 132.

The anecdotal accounts of Juan and Vincent are not new to writing program administrators (WPAs). Their placement experiences are a single pattern, or at least two overlapping ones: a student takes mainstream composition but is then steered by a teacher away from English 102 because it has been discovered that the student is a multilingual writer. It seems that the students were sort of aimless and passive, being moved around by various authority figures at their universities, when questions we should really be asking are what the students themselves want, how they can make well-informed placement decisions, and exercise their own agency in their placement decisions instead of just doing what others tell them. As yet, we have lacked empirical evidence to explain such placement experiences as well as the placement of multilingual students into college composition courses in particular.

Second language (L2) writing research and writing studies discussion on first-year composition placement has informed us about and allowed us to understand multilingual writers' placement perceptions and their preferences for enrolling in multilingual composition over mainstream composition or vice versa (e.g., Braine 1996; Chiang and Schmida 1999; Harklau 2000; Costino and Hyon 2007; Ortmeier-Hooper 2008; Ruecker 2011). Yet, as WPAs continue to determine appropriate placement for multilingual students in order to meet their differing needs, what is learned from research into placement preferences and perceptions may not be sufficient. One main reason is that we have neglected to understand *how* multilingual students make decisions about placement into mainstream or multilingual composition courses. As illustrated by the cases of Juan and Vincent, we do not know *how* they ended up being in English 101 and *what* went into their placement decision process, among others. Students' placement decisions, I argue, are fundamental and need to be fully examined, mainly because those decisions can determine students' "success or failure" (Braine 1996, 91) in first-year college writing courses.

This book demonstrates why looking at students' placement decisions is an important element for developing and improving placement practices for multilingual writers in college composition programs. It primarily explores how multilingual students exercise *agency* in their placement decisions and how *student agency* can inform the overall programmatic placement of multilingual students in college composition programs. Specifically, the book follows 11 multilingual students who made their decisions about placement into mainstream or multilingual first-year composition courses over the course of one academic year at ASU, a large public university located in the Southwest of the United States. It argues why we need to understand multilingual students' placement decision-making process more clearly and describes how we should use what we have learned about that process to improve placement practices for multilingual students, particularly how we advise students about placement.

I focus on the placement decisions of multilingual writers because these writers are regularly presenting in institutions of US higher education. According to the Institute of International

Education (IIE)'s "2015 Open Doors Report on International Educational Exchange" released on November 16, 2015, "the number of international students at U.S. colleges and universities had the highest rate of growth in 35 years, increasing by ten percent to a record high of 974, 926 students in the 2014/2015 academic year" ("2015 Open Doors Report on International Educational Exchange" 2015). With this sharply increasing number of international multilingual students, plus a regular presence of resident multilingual students[3] in college composition programs, it is essential that WPAs and writing teachers take "responsibility for the regular presence of second language writers in writing classes, to understand their characteristics, and *to develop* instructional and *administrative practices that are sensitive to their linguistic and cultural needs*" (CCCC Statement on Second Language Writing and Writers 2009, para. 4; emphasis mine). My research is conducted with multilingual writers at one institution; yet I believe the placement issues examined here are relevant to other student populations, including multilingual and monolingual, in other contexts and settings.

The rest of this chapter develops exigencies of my research and lays the groundwork for the subsequent chapters: establishing the significance of students' placement decisions; proposing a definition of agency developed from a synthesis of existing discussions of theory of agency and my own research data; and examining different placement methods and their relation to student agency. A theory of agency I develop will be illustrated through the stories of the 11 multilingual writers in the remainder of this book and elaborated in chapter 7. The last part of this current chapter introduces the research context and participants and ends with an overview of the remaining chapters.

WHY MULTILINGUAL STUDENTS' PLACEMENT DECISIONS?

One of my main goals as a WPA, like other WPAs, is to ensure appropriate course placement for students' success in writing courses. We have pondered over placement-related questions like how placement should be decided, what method should be used, and how placement outcomes should be assessed. In the meantime, as Marcia Lee Ribble (2002) points out, "more and more composition programs are looking at their placement practices as inadequate to explain student failure. There have been a number of attempts to increase student success and student retention, by developing placement practices that are directly linked to improved writing pedagogies" (13).

One such attempt includes adopting various placement methods in order to guarantee placement that can meet students' learning and writing needs. These placement methods are: standardized test scores (indirect assessment), a single timed-writing sample (direct assessment), portfolios, and directed self-placement (Peckham 2009). A combination of these methods has also been used in many writing programs, such as standardized test scores and a timed-writing essay, or standardized test scores and directed self-placement (Huot 1994; Williams 1995; Peckham 2009). Placement methods vary from institution to institution based on institutional contexts and local needs. Writing programs use these placement methods to place students, including multilingual students, into different first-year composition course options. Particularly, there are four placement options, as described by Tony Silva (1994), for multilingual students. The first option is to place multilingual writers in mainstream composition classes with native users of English. Another approach is to create a separate section of first-year composition designated for multilingual writers. It is possible that multilingual writers can be placed in the same class with native English-speaking basic writers who need extra time to develop their academic writing skills. Multilingual students can also be placed in a cross-cultural composition class in which a more or less equal number of native English-speaking students and non-native English-speaking students are systematically integrated (see a more nuanced discussion in Matsuda and Silva 1999; see also Jordan 2012; Miller-Cochran 2012).

The placement itself is complex. Placement is made even more complicated by conflicting results of research (Sullivan and Nielsen 2009) that has looked into multilingual students' placement perceptions and preferences (Braine 1996; Chiang and Schmida 1999; Costino and Hyon 2007; Ortmeier-Hooper 2008). To illustrate, George Braine's (1996) study showed that a majority of ESL students (international and resident non-native English students) preferred to enroll in ESL classes to mainstream classes. The study also reported that students who enrolled in ESL classes performed better in an exit exam than those enrolled in mainstream sections. A study by Kimberly Costino and Sunny Hyon echoes Braine's conclusion that L2 students prefer ESL writing classes (Costino and Hyon 2007). In the Costino and Hyon study, international students and US-born resident immigrants preferred the multilingual section. One possible reason might be that they felt comfortable working with their non-native English-speaking friends who were like them. Another reason might be the teachers, who were well trained and knew how to work effectively with them. Contrarily, L2 students (US resident L2 students referred to as Generation 1.5 students) in a study by Yuet-Sim Chiang and Mary Schmida resisted being in ESL writing classes because they did not associate themselves with the ESL label of those first-year composition sections (Chiang and Schmida 1999). Like the US resident L2 students in Chiang and Schmida's (1999) study, an ESL immigrant student in a study by Christina Ortmeier-Hooper (2008) did not like being "classified as an 'ESL' student" (397). This student chose to be enrolled in an honors section of first-year composition and ignored an ESL section because he did not consider himself to be an ESL student. These situations are likely to happen, as Linda Blanton (1999) points out, because when US resident L2 students "reach college, they may feel strongly that they shouldn't be placed differently from other U.S. high school graduates, and are offended when labeled *ESL*" (123; emphasis in original).

In summary, these conflicting placement preferences and perceptions make it more difficult to understand the placement of multilingual writers into first-year composition courses. This book is an attempt to build this understanding, and I hope to do so through the stories of the 11 multilingual writers who made their decisions about placement into mainstream or multilingual first-year composition courses.

AGENCY: A THEORETICAL FRAMEWORK

Before presenting an operationalized definition of agency, I address different views about agency and so argue that there is no consensus on agency. What is currently known is just a bewildering array of competing definitions. To begin, let's consider general definitions of agency, which involve an act. Anthropologist Laura Ahearn (2001) defines agency as follows: "Agency is the socioculturally mediated capacity to act," and she considers it to be a "provisional definition" (122). For British Marxist historian and writer Perry Anderson (1980), agency is a "conscious, goal-directed activity" (19). In my view, there is a link between agency and action, but this idea is complicated by other developing definitions of agency (I discuss this complication in the following paragraphs). As a result, it makes agency tricky and difficult to define; this seems to be in agreement in both applied linguistics and rhetoric studies (Hauser 2004; van Lier 2009).

In applied linguistics, Leo van Lier, among others, notes that a delineation of agency is "far from straightforward" (van Lier 2009, xii), and it is difficult to make a distinction between agency and autonomy and other related constructs, including self and identity. According to van Lier, if "self is basically anything and everything we call 'me' or 'I'" (Harter 1999, quoted in van Lier 2009, x), agency, which involves an act, can be equally looked at from the two ends of a continuum. On one end, "agency refers to the ways in which, and the extents to which, the person (self, identities, and all) is compelled to, motivated to, allowed to, and coerced to, *act*" (van Lier 2009, x; emphasis in original). On the other end, "agency refers equally to the person deciding to, wanting to, insisting to, agreeing to, and negotiating to, *act*" (van Lier 2009, x; emphasis in original). These definitions of agency by van Lier capture "nicely the complexities of the notion of agency" (van Lier 2009, x).

In rhetoric, Gerard Hauser (2004) suggests that there are divergences of what constitutes agency, and how it should be conceptualized. These divergences, however, have led to various developing definitions of agency and each has emphasized differing features of agency. For example, Amanda Young (2008), based on results of her study of teenage girls who were interacting with a computer program about safe sex, describes that "agency entails planning and decision-making. It also requires self-evaluation and the recognition of internal and external expertise. Agency is constructed and expressed in how people manage conflicts and design plans for change that acknowledge people's beliefs and readiness to change behavior if warranted" (244).

Young also suggests the fundamental properties of agency, which include questioning, negotiation, choice, and evaluation (228). For other scholars, these properties are considered to be resources for agency (e.g., Callinicos 1988, 236; Flannery 1991, 702). Nick Turnbull (2004) considers agency to be a property of questioning and suggests the following: "Where there is choice there is agency" (207). Kathryn Flannery (1991) takes a step further and comments that "choice is itself a resource to which agents have different access" (702); and agents can choose not to make use of resources that are out there. Flannery also notes that it is agents who "possess the potential to act or not act contingent upon their 'relative access to productive resources'" (Callinicos 1988, 236, quoted in Flannery 1991, 702).

Karlyn Campbell (2005), based on her analysis of the text created by a white woman 12 years after Sojourner Truth's speech in 1851, proposes that agency "(1) is communal and participatory, hence, both constituted and constrained by externals that are material and symbolic; (2) is 'invented' by authors who are points of articulations; (3) emerges in artistry or craft; (4) is effected through form; (5) is perverse, that is, inherently, protean, ambiguous, open to reversal" (2).

The notion of agency, as asserted by Amy Koerber (2006), has a component of resistance. This claim of Koerber is built from her technical communication analysis of interviews with breastfeeding advocates who support breastfeeding mothers and assist them when they encounter problems. Koerber's interviewees said that mothers had to resist other elements of medical discourse and cultural perceptions that contradicted official medical guidelines on breastfeeding. Mothers' acts of resistance, as Koerber suggests, are "the kind of rhetorical negotiation that might be construed as the occupation of preexisting subject positions rather than true resistance" (88). More important, the acts, in the context of this study, "begin as active selection among discursive alternatives" (88).

Operationalized Definition of Agency

I maintain the idea of the link between agency and acts. I also see that there must be factors that make agency possible and so consider such factors to be conditions for agency. In the interest of multilingual students' placement decisions, I develop an operationalized definition of agency, employing it as a theoretical lens to understand student agency and how it can help improve placement practices for multilingual students in college composition courses. My operationalized definition of agency reads as follows: *Agency is the capacity to act or not to act, contingent upon various conditions.*

In the context of this book, conditions for agency include freedom to choose writing courses and information about placement that was distributed through the following sources: academic advisors' recommendations, other students' past experiences in taking first-year composition courses, new student orientation, and other sources that provided placement related information (see appendix C). I developed these constructs during the process of data analysis and of writing this book.

I should also note that the capacity to act with respect to placement in a first-year writing course is valuable—even if, for instance, it opens up the risk that a student might make a poor placement decision, by overestimating her/his writing skills, taking a particular course for social rather than academic reasons (see Crusan 2006 in the next pages).

PLACEMENT METHODS AND STUDENT AGENCY

I discussed earlier that writing programs, varying from institution to institution, place students into writing courses using different placement methods, including standardized test scores (indirect assessment), a single timed-writing sample (direct assessment), portfolios, and directed self-placement (Peckham 2009). A combination of these methods has also been used in many writing programs such as standardized test scores and a timed-writing essay (Huot 1994; Williams 1995; Peckham 2009). My goal in the next pages is to critically review some of the major findings of research on assessment and placement in order to demonstrate a relationship between placement methods and student agency. In the end, I argue that these placement methods work against or interfere with student agency.

Research has told us that timed-writing essays and standardized test scores are the most widely used methods to determine placement for students. To illustrate, results of Brian Huot's (1994) nationwide survey of writing placement practices of 1,037 public and private institutions indicated that a timed-writing sample was the most widely used placement method (51%), followed by standardized test scores (ACT or SAT) (42%), and a combination of a timed-writing essay and standardized test scores (23%). Huot's survey echoed a previous study by Karen Greenberg, Harvey Wiener, and Richard Donovan, which demonstrated that the majority of institutions used a placement essay to determine English placement (Greenberg, Wiener, and Donovan 1986). On the contrary, Jessica Williams's (1995) nationwide survey of 78 colleges and universities showed that direct assessment like a placement essay (23%) was not as widely used as indirect assessment (58%) for deciding placement for ESL students, when combining the percentages of an institutionally administered indirect test (32%) and TOEFL scores (26%). A combination of standardized test scores and a timed-writing essay was also found (19%).

The use of timed-writing samples or placement essays versus the use of standardized test scores for placement has long been a heated discussion in placement and assessment. Advocates for direct assessment like the National Testing Network in Writing and the National Council of Teachers of English recommend using timed-writing samples for placing students into writing courses (Gordon 1987). This practice is also preferred by language assessment specialists (e.g., White 1994, quoted in Crusan 2002; Ferretti 2001; Crusan and Cornett 2002) who advocate essay tests because "they are able to gauge the ability of students to identify and analyze problems, to identify audience and purpose, to argue, describe, and define, skills that are valued in composition classes in the United States" (Crusan 2002, 19). Yet research has shown that the use of a timed-writing sample "has been defined as preferable if only one measure for placement into composition courses will be used, and if the only alternative is a multiple-choice test" (Matzen and Hoyt 2004, 3). Multiple-choice tests have been criticized because they "isolate and evaluate knowledge of specific components of language" (Crusan 2002, 19).

Supporters of the use of standardized test scores like Barbara Gordon argue that "standardized tests are more accurate than a single writing sample for placing students," explaining that "[. . .] with regard to validity and reliability, a single writing sample is among the most unacceptable means to place students" (Gordon 1987, 29). Other advocates for standardized test scores also question the reliability and validity of writing samples' results (e.g., Huot 1990; Belanoff 1991; Elbow 1997). While Hunter Breland (1977) points out that a writing sample is not a useful indicator of a student's writing ability compared to an objective assessment, Pearl Saunders (2000) suggests that writing samples are not necessary for accurate placement. Because of the limitations of both timed-writing essays and standardized test scores, assessment specialists (e.g., Leki 1991; Haswell 1998; Crusan 2002) have considered other strategies for placing students into writing courses. Deborah Crusan (2002), for example, particularly recommends using multiple instruments (a combination of direct and indirect assessment) as a means to place multilingual writers into first-year writing courses.

The use of portfolios is another placement method employed in US writing programs. In this placement means, high school teachers help students develop their portfolios before submitting them to writing programs at particular institutions for assessment. Since the portfolio system is impractical for international and out-of-state students, it has not been widely used as the placement method for international students (P. K. Matsuda, pers. comm.)

In view of the limitations of standardized test scores, placement essays, and portfolios, the implementation of an alternative placement method called directed self-placement (DSP) at Grand Valley State University (Royer and Gilles 1998, 2003) attracted the attention of several writing programs nationwide. DSP informs students about appropriate and accurate information on available first-year writing courses as well as advantages and disadvantages of taking those courses. Since Royer and Gilles's groundbreaking article, "Directed Self-Placement: An Attitude of Orientation," appeared in *College Composition and Communication* in 1998, many institutions have become interested in DSP and have adopted it as a placement procedure in lieu of traditional placement methods. Since DSP refuses to make placement decisions for students, it fosters student agency by forcing students to choose a writing course they believe is right for them.

Royer and Gilles discuss DSP in the context of first language (L1) composition. In the context of second language (L2) writing, the use of DSP as a placement method originally excludes L2 writers (Crusan 2006). As explained by Crusan (2006), resistance to an inclusion of L2 writers in DSP by her L2 writing colleagues stems from their beliefs that L2 students are prone to make poor decisions about their language proficiency. L2 writers, some believe, either overestimate or underestimate themselves; as a consequence, they may place themselves into a course that is above or below their level of proficiency. In contrast, a study by Diane Strong-Krause (2000) suggests that L2 students will be able to self-evaluate if self-assessment instruments are carefully developed and appropriately implemented.

It has been argued that DSP probably comes with disadvantages if students are not well informed about writing courses that are available to them and about advantages and disadvantages of taking those courses. Furthermore, in a situation in which students cannot make appropriate decisions about placement, they may end up being in a writing course that does not fit their writing ability and proficiency. As pointed out by Ellen Schendel and Peggy O'Neill, "directed self-placement may not work in some contexts, as students may misjudge their writing abilities" (Schendel and O'Neill 1999, 218). Schendel and O'Neill base their criticism on psychological research by Justin Kruger and David Dunning, which suggests that undergraduate students tend to misjudge their performance and they do not necessarily possess self-evaluation skills when they first arrive at college (Kruger and Dunning 1999).

To mitigate these probable disadvantages of DSP as a placement method, Cynthia Lewiecki-Wilson, Jeff Sommers, and John Paul Tassoni from Miami University, Middletown campus (an open-admissions institution) create a writing placement process called the Writer's Profile in which students are engaged in "self-reflection and teachers incorporate knowledge gained into their classrooms and curricula" (Lewiecki-Wilson, Sommers, and Tassoni 2000, 172), but in the end teachers are the ones who decide course placement for students. For Lewiecki-Wilson, Sommers, and Tassoni, "the best placement decisions would be reached both through student self-reflection *and* assessment from those [teachers] who know the curriculum" (168; emphasis in original).

Building on the previous work by Kathleen Yancey (1992) and Rhonda Grego and Nancy Thompson (1995, 1996), the Writer's Profile, which is developed based on the same concept of portfolios, consists of multiple types of student writing such as lists, notes, drafts, and revisions (Grego and Thompson 1995, 1996). Students work on their Writer's Profile at home and self-select pieces of writing to include in the profile. Two writing teachers evaluate the Writer's Profile. When an agreement is reached, course placement is suggested to each student. In the Writer's Profile, students are asked to complete multiple tasks. In the prewriting stage, students are first asked to write down the first thing that comes into their head about all of the writing they have done in the last month or so. Second, they are asked to respond to a different question about the writing they have done in school. Third, they respond to another question about writing in college, particularly their goals for writing in college and about what they think writing in college will be like. In the drafting stage, students use the information they have from their prewriting to compose a two- to three-page Writer's Profile, a portrait of themselves as writers. Lewiecki-Wilson, Sommers, and Tassoni (2000) believe that the Writer's Profile can help students and their advisors "make more informed choices about course placement" (166) because both students' actual writing and teachers' placement recommendations are used to decide course placement for students. A rationale behind the Writer's Profile, as noted by Lewiecki-Wilson, Sommers, and Tassoni is that "placement should not be something we do to or *for* students, but something we do *with* students" (173; emphasis in original).

In the final analysis, when writing programs or institutions use standardized test scores, timed-writing samples, and portfolios, they all use scores to determine placement for students. Clearly, these three placement methods do not seem to allow room for student agency unless students study hard and decide to retake a test for a better score—this applies to the use of standardized test scores as a placement method. DSP and the Writer's Profile are different; they are designed to maximize student agency. As I discussed earlier, while DSP grants full agency to students and believes that placement should be a student's own choice (Royer and Gilles 1998), the Writer's Profile allows students to act as agents who self-reflect on their writing; writing teachers assess students' reflections and decide an appropriate writing course for them (Lewiecki-Wilson, Sommers, and Tassoni 2000).

Systematically, DSP presents conditions for agency by providing placement information and placement options to students;

in the end students are the ones who get to decide what writing course they will take. It is clear that conditions for agency are built into the DSP system. In the use of standardized test scores, conditions for agency are not built into its system. Yet, it does not mean that agency cannot or does not exist in the system of standardized test scores when various placement options are made available to students and students have the freedom to choose writing courses. This book explores, among other things, how conditions for agency are distributed in the context of (many) typical US writing programs where test scores are used as a means to place multilingual students into first-year composition courses.

THE RESEARCH CONTEXT

This research was conducted in the writing program at ASU between Fall 2010 and Spring 2011. Recognized as one of the largest writing programs in the country, the writing program enrolls both native users of English and multilingual students. Housed in the English Department, the writing program offers a variety of placement options for first-year composition courses.[4] There are two main tracks of first-year composition: mainstream and multilingual. Each track has different levels of first-year writing courses, ranging from developmental to advanced composition, for students to choose from. Table 1.1 shows the placement options that are available to students.

For the mainstream track, the writing program offers the two-semester first-year writing sequence (ENG 101 and ENG 102), the stretch first-year writing course (WAC 101),[5] which stretches the first-year writing course (ENG 101) over two semesters, and the advanced composition (ENG 105), which is a one semester writing course that can satisfy the first-year writing requirement. For the multilingual track, the writing program offers the two-semester first-year writing sequence (ENG 107 and ENG 108), which is equivalent to ENG 101 and ENG 102. Like WAC 101, WAC 107 stretches the first-year writing course (ENG 107) over two semesters.

Table 1.1. Placement Options

	Mainstream	Multilingual
Advanced Composition	ENG 105	No course offered
First-Year Composition II	ENG 102	ENG 108 (English for Foreign Students*)
First-Year Composition I	ENG 101	ENG 107 (English for Foreign Students*)
Stretch Composition	WAC 101 (Introduction to Academic Writing)	WAC 107 ((Introduction to Academic Writing for Foreign Students*)

*Beginning in Fall 2012, the course title of ENG 107 and ENG 108 was changed to First-Year Composition and that of WAC 107 was changed to Introduction to Academic Writing.

The writing program places students into first-year writing courses using standardized test scores, such as SAT, ACT, TOEFL, and IELTS. In a situation that students do not have test scores or are not satisfied with their test scores, they have an option to take the Accuplacer Test (The WritePlacer section), a placement test for a first-year English course administered by the University Testing and Scanning Services. Students can take this test only once. Table 1.2 shows test score cutoff points and course placement.[6]

Placement information is communicated to students by academic advisors. Incoming students meet their academic advisors before each fall semester starts during new student orientation, which takes place between March and early July. Students register for classes, including a first-year writing class, during the orientation. Some international students holding student visas register for classes online, including a first-year writing class, when they are in their home countries. They contact academic advisors via email asking for advice on enrollment. Others wait until they arrive to campus and register. Communication about placement information to international students is minimal. They primarily rely on recommendations from academic advisors. Before and during the time of this research (Fall 2010–Spring 2011), there had been no formal communication about first-year composition placement between the writing program and writing teachers.

Table 1.2. Test Scores and Course Placement

Placement Exam	Score	Course
SAT Verbal	460 and below	WAC 101 or 107
ACT English	18 or below	WAC 101 or 107
Accuplacer	7 or below (12-point system) / 4 or below (8-point system, effective Fall 2009)	WAC 101 or WAC 107
TOEFL	Below 560PBT/220CBT/83iBT	WAC 107
SAT Verbal	470–610	ENG 101 or ENG 107
ACT English	19–25	ENG 101 or ENG 107
Accuplacer	8–10 (12-point system) / 5–7 (8-point system, effective Fall 2009)	ENG 101 or ENG 107
TOEFL	560PBT/220CBT/83iBT and above	ENG 101 or ENG 107
SAT Verbal	620 or more	ENG 105
ACT English	26 or more	ENG 105
Accuplacer	11 or more (12-point system) / 8 (8-point system, effective Fall 2009)	ENG 105

In each fall semester, the writing program offers about five hundred or more sections of writing courses—this includes first-year writing courses and other higher-level writing courses for undergraduate students. For each spring semester, the number of sections is reduced to about four hundred sections or so. During the time of this research, the writing program offered 426 sections of first-year composition courses (out of 544 sections of all writing courses) in Fall 2010. The total number of students enrolled in first-year writing course was 8,258. In Spring 2011, 322 sections (out of 443 sections of all writing courses) of first-year writing courses were offered. The total number of students was 5,867.

I should note that the ASU writing program has two WPAs: Director of Writing Programs and Director of Second Language Writing. While the former is in charge of the mainstream composition, the latter is in charge of multilingual composition.

RESEARCH DESIGN

I conducted an interview-based qualitative study (see appendix B for interview questions) in the studied writing program over the course of one academic year (Fall 2010–Spring 2011). The goal was to address the primary research questions as follows:

1. How do multilingual writers make the decisions about placement into mainstream or multilingual first-year composition courses?

2. How do multilingual writers exercise agency in their placement decisions?

3. What is the role of academic advisors and writing teachers regarding multilingual writers' placement decisions?

4. How can the placement policy/procedure be developed in order to maximize student agency?

I carried out a series of four in-depth interviews informed by Irving Seidman's (2006) model called "in-depth, phenomenologically based interviewing" (15) with 11 multilingual undergraduate writers from various language backgrounds. I interviewed each of the students two times in Fall 2010 and two more times in Spring 2011. In this interview approach, open-ended questions are used in order to encourage participants to reconstruct their experience under the topic of the study. In my research, I used semi-structured questions, which I found helpful for students when they did not have anything to say. The questions helped both the students and me continue the conversation. I often asked follow-up questions that were not listed. This type of interview allowed me to closely follow individual multilingual writers, which helped me understand each of them thoroughly. It also allowed me to understand why they did what they did. From the first interview to the fourth interview, the student participants became more comfortable sharing with me their English placement experiences. Information gained from each interview helped develop an understanding of each student's whole placement decision processes and what went into their decisions about taking first-year writing courses.

I also carried out one-time interviews with some of the multilingual student participants' academic advisors and writing
teachers to gain their perspectives on the placement of multilingual writers into college composition courses. Furthermore,
I interviewed the director of Writing Programs and the director
of Second Language Writing twice in order to obtain information about the writing program's placement policies and other
related issues, as well as information about changes that have
been made to the placement policies after my research was
completed. In addition to the interviews, I examined online
information related to first-year English composition placement
from the English Department's website, the writing program's
website, the university's new student orientation 2010 website,
and the University Testing and Scanning Services' website. I also
collected related documents, such as major maps and DARS
(Degree Audit Reporting System).[7]

After completion of data collection, I informally analyzed
interview transcripts at a transcribing stage where summaries
and notes were typed. Formal analysis began when the transcripts were coded. Coding and data analysis (see appendix
C) was guided by the operationalized definition of agency discussed earlier. The theory of agency that I developed was used
as a theoretical lens when analyzing student interview data. My
coding and data analysis was also guided by the established
research questions. I was also open for emerging themes and
patterns. Data analysis was a recursive process, and it continued
throughout the process of writing this book.

Meet the Participants

Multilingual Students

The 11 multilingual students (see appendix A) participating in my research came from various language backgrounds,
countries, and disciplines. They included two US citizens, two
permanent residents, and seven international visa students;
five females, six males; aged eighteen to thirty when they
first enrolled at ASU; from the United States, China, Norway,

Kazakhstan, the United Arab Emirates, and Qatar; studying political science, industrial engineering, mechanical engineering, computer information systems, business communication, business management, economics, mathematics and statistics, and mathematics and film. While two student participants were enrolled in mainstream composition sections, the rest were enrolled in multilingual composition sections. Following are the brief introductions of the multilingual student participants with their pseudonyms, test scores, and English course placement. This information is summarized in table 1.3. Other detailed descriptions of each student participant are enriched in chapters 3–5 when I present the student case studies.

- *Jasim* is a 19-year-old visa student from Dubai, the United Arab Emirates (UAE). He scored 6.5 on IELTS and was enrolled in ENG 107 and ENG 108, respectively.

- *Joel* is a 30-year-old US permanent resident from Mexico. He scored 542 on PBT (paper-based test) TOEFL. He took WAC 107, followed by ENG 107 and ENG 108, respectively.

- *Marco* is an 18-year-old US citizen from Mexico. He scored 480 on SAT Verbal and registered for ENG 101 and ENG 102, respectively.

- *Chan* is a 22-year-old visa student from China. She scored 90 on the iBT (Internet-based test) TOEFL and registered for ENG 107 and ENG 108, respectively.

- *Jonas*[8] is a visa student from Norway. He scored 77 on iBT and was originally placed into WAC 107. He took the Accuplacer Test and scored 5 out of 8 on the WritePlacer section and was able to take ENG 107.

- *Afia* is a 22-year-old US permanent resident from Qatar. She scored 76 on iBT TOEFL and was originally placed into WAC 107. She took the Accuplacer Test and scored 5 and was able to enroll in ENG 107.

- *Pascal* is a 20-year-old visa student originally from France. He scored 102 on iBT TOEFL and was enrolled in ENG 107 and ENG 108, respectively.

- *Mei* is a 20-year-old visa student from China. She scored 6.5 on IELTS and was enrolled in ENG 107, followed by ENG 108.

- *Ana* is an 18-year-old US citizen student from the United States. She scored 26 on her ACT English; with this score,

Table 1.3 Multilingual Student Participants

Student	Country / native language	Length of time in the US	Age	Residency status	Test score	Course placement
Jasim	United Arab Emirates / Arabic	Almost 2 years	19	International visa student	6.5 (IELTS)	ENG 107 and 108
Joel	Mexico / Spanish	3 years	30	US permanent resident (from marriage)	542 (TOEFL PBT)	WAC 107, ENG 107 and 108
Marco	Mexico / Spanish	13 years	18	US citizen	480 (SAT Verbal)	ENG 101 and 102
Chan	China / Chinese	Almost 1 year	22	International visa student	90 (TOEFL iBT)	ENG 107 and 108
Jonas	Norway / Norwegian	2 months	NA	International visa student	77 (TOEFL iBT)	ENG 107 and 108
Afia	Qatar / Arabic	1.5 years	22	US permanent resident	76 (TOEFL iBT)	ENG 107 and 108
Pascal	France / French	9 months	20	International visa student	102 (TOEFL iBT)	ENG 107 and 108
Mei	China / Chinese	7 months	20	International visa student	6.5 (IELTS)	ENG 107 and 108
Ana	United States / Spanish	Entire life (18 years)	18	US citizen	26 (ACT English)	ENG 101 and 102
Askar	Kazakhstan / Kazakh	3 years	19	International visa student	96 (TOEFL iBT)	107 and 108
Ting	China / Chinese	8 months	20	International visa student	84 (TOEFL iBT)	ENG 107 and 108

she could enroll in ENG 105. Ana, however, registered for ENG 101 and ENG 102, respectively.

- *Askar* is a 19-year-old visa student from Kazakhstan. He scored 96 on iBT TOEFL and was enrolled in ENG 107 and ENG 108, respectively.

- *Ting* is a 20-year-old visa student from China. She scored 84 on iBT TOEFL and was enrolled in ENG 107 and ENG 108, respectively.

Academic Advisors

The four academic advisors were full-time academic advisors (non-faculty advisors) from electrical engineering, business administration, mathematics and statistics, and economics. They were academic advisors of some of the multilingual student participants. They were two males and two females; they had years of advising experience ranging from two to six years. Each had a few years of experience in working with multilingual students at this institution. Below is their brief background information:

- *Jerry* is an academic advisor for electrical engineering majors. He has six years of advising experience.
- *Keith* is an academic advisor for business administration students and has worked with a few multilingual students in the past.
- *Elaine* is an academic advisor for economics majors and has five years of experience in student advising. She has also taught economics for undergraduate students at the same time.
- *Megan* is an academic advisor for mathematics and statistics majors and has two years of advising experience.

Writing Teachers

Like the academic advisor participants, the five writing teachers were instructors of the focal multilingual students. Two taught both mainstream and multilingual composition, two taught only multilingual composition, and one taught only mainstream composition. Two were graduate teaching assistants, two were full-time instructors, and one was an adjunct instructor. While two writing teachers never had L2 writing training, the rest did. Their experience in teaching in the writing program ranged from three years to almost 10 years. Their information is as follows:

- *Beverly* is an adjunct instructor. She taught two sections of ENG 107, two sections of ENG 108, and one section of ENG 102 in Fall 2010. Throughout her three years at this institution, she has had experience teaching both multilingual and mainstream composition. She earned a master's degree in TESOL and used to tutor non-native English speakers.

- *Sammy* is a full-time instructor, and she taught two sections of ENG 107 and two sections of ENG 105 in Fall 2010. For almost 10 years, she has been teaching both multilingual and mainstream composition in the writing program. Sammy earned a PhD in English. She used to teach English at the university level in Japan for nine years. When she returned to the United States, she began privately tutoring international multilingual students. She never had L2 writing training but learned to teach L2 writing in the classroom.

- *Anne*, a doctoral student in rhetoric, composition, and linguistics, is a graduate teaching assistant and taught two sections of ENG 107 in Fall 2010. A fifth year TA, she had taught both mainstream and multilingual composition. Prior to coming to ASU, she had L2 writing training and taught English speaking in India and at a university in Portland.

- *Ethan*, a doctoral student in rhetoric, composition, and linguistics, is a graduate teaching assistant and taught two sections of ENG 107 in Fall 2010. He earned a master's degree in TESOL and had L2 writing training.

- *Dan* is a full-time instructor and taught five sections of ENG 101 in Fall 2010. He earned a PhD in English Education. Over the past six years (the first three years as a teaching assistant and the rest as an instructor) of teaching in the writing program, Dan has taught only mainstream composition. He did have experience in teaching multilingual students, but it was minimal. He has never received L2 writing training.

ORGANIZATION OF THE BOOK

The rest of the book takes a more descriptive or narrative approach to providing readers with detailed portraits of the focal multilingual writers' first-year composition placement experiences over the course of one academic year, particularly focusing on their placement decisions. Like Ilona Leki (2007), I intend to "leave maximum room for these students' voices and [placement] experiences" (13) and keep "to a minimum outside scholarly references" (13). Because I want to let my multilingual writers voice out their placement stories, the remaining chapters primarily rely on direct quotes from a series of four in-depth interviews. I understand that "this choice makes it more difficult for readers to come away from the narratives with 'the point,'" but "it helps the narratives remain somewhat truer to the students' experiences" (Leki 2007, 13). However, from time to time, I will shift from descriptive data to my analytical discussion. It is also my intention not to edit the interview excerpts.

Chapter 2 is the heart of the book, providing a fundamental understanding of how multilingual students make their placement decisions. The chapter examines various sources of placement information—academic advisors' recommendations, other students' past placement experiences, new student orientation, and other sources providing placement-related information—exploited by the focal multilingual students when they chose to enroll in a mainstream or multilingual composition course. These sources of placement information, as I argue throughout the book, are conditions that make student agency in placement decisions possible. In other words, when these conditions are optimal, multilingual students will be able to exercise their agency, having the capacity to *negotiate* placement, *accept* or *deny* placement, *self-asses* their proficiency as they choose a writing course, *plan for* and *question* placement.

I call these capacities *acts of agency*, and I highlight them in the following three theme-based chapters (3–5), which are organized around the seven case studies. Each chapter will begin with a detailed description of the focal multilingual students' profiles, followed by a discussion of their first-year placement experiences, scrutinizing what went into their placement decision process and the act(s) of agency they performed. These theme-based chapters also examine what happened after the placement decisions were made; and the goal is to illustrate the entire decision-making process rather than the outcome of the placement decisions. The cases of Afia and Joel in chapter

3 delineate the acts of negotiating and accepting placement. Chapter 4 explicates the act of self-assessing, demonstrating why and how self-evaluation was crucial for Jonas and Pascal when they were choosing their first-year writing courses. Chapter 5 showcases the acts of planning and questioning in which Jasim, Chan, and Ting found helpful while they were in the process of making placement decisions, particularly in their second semester. This chapter also explores emerging conditions for agency and succeeding acts of agency, delineating what caused such conditions and acts of agency.

Chapters 6 and 7 look into two other important placement stakeholders: academic advisors and writing teachers. Drawing on the discussion in chapter 2, especially how recommendations from academic advisors were the primary source of the focal students' placement decisions, chapter 6 examines the roles of academic advising in multilingual students' first-year composition placement decisions. Readers will also find voices of the focal multilingual students, who share their views and comments on English placement advising. This chapter's arrangement is appropriate because it is impossible to discuss a complete picture of English course placement advising without including students' perspectives or vice versa. Chapter 7's premise is that writing teachers work closely with students, yet we lack an understanding of how much writing teachers know about placement practices of multilingual students. This chapter asks what roles writing teachers should play in the placement of multilingual students in college composition programs and considers ways in which writing programs can involve writing teachers in the placement procedures for multilingual students.

Drawing on the discussions in previous chapters, chapter 8 explores how student agency can inform the overall programmatic placement of multilingual students, highlighting programmatic concerns and research implications for WPAs as they continue to improve the placement practices for multilingual writers. I also articulate my theory of agency and scrutinize how it can be applied in other situations. The book ends with a coda in which I report on changes that have been made in the studied writing program after my research was completed. I also share some placement-related documents, including a placement brochure and placement handout, I developed as a result of this research. The studied writing program has used these documents since June 2012.

NOTES

1. This research was conducted at Arizona State University. While the name of the institution is revealed, the students, writing teachers, and academic advisors mentioned in the book are identified by pseudonyms.

2. I used the term "multilingual writers" in this book to refer to "a wide range of students who are actively developing proficiency in the English language" (Matsuda, Saenkhum, and Accardi 2013, 73). I chose to use this term because "it seemed to be the most widely accepted euphemism for L2 writers" (Matsuda, Saenkhum, and Accardi 2013, 73) in the context of US college composition programs during the time of conducting this research and writing this book. Other terms like ESL, L2, and Generation 1.5 will also be seen in the book when referring to previous studies in which these terms were originally used.

3. Identifying resident multilingual students has been difficult (Harklau 2000, 36). When these students enter US colleges and universities, institutions do not collect information about their language backgrounds due to their status of US citizens or residents.

4. In addition to first-year composition courses, the writing program offers other higher-level English courses for undergraduate students.

5. Stretch Composition (WAC 101 and WAC 107) is designed to help develop students' academic writing skills. Students have more time to work on their writing until they are ready to take the regular first-year writing sequence (ENG 101 and ENG 102 or ENG 107 and ENG 108). For detailed descriptions of Stretch Composition, see Glau 2007.

6. Information in table 1.2 had been used for placement before and during the time of this research was conducted between Fall 2010 and Spring 2011. For more updated information, visit https://english.clas.asu.edu /admission/first-year-composition-courses/placement-information.

7. DARS (Degree Audit Reporting System) is available through MyASU, the university's online system in which students have access to their classes, specific courses they are enrolled, and other resources.

8. Since Jonas did not show up after his first two interviews completed, I did not have information about his age and other related information because I collected information about the student participants' backgrounds in the final interview.

2
INVESTIGATING MULTILINGUAL WRITERS' PLACEMENT DECISIONS

. . . but placement ought to be a student's own choice.

—Royer and Gilles (1998, 65)

Current L2 writing research on first-year composition placement (e.g., Braine 1996; Chiang and Schmida 1999; Harklau 2000; Costino and Hyon 2007; Ortmeier-Hooper 2008; Ruecker 2011) has provided an understanding of why multilingual writers preferred separate L2 writing sections of composition courses over mainstream sections or vice versa. This area of research has also described multilingual students' perceptions of placement practices in general. Yet, as we continue to develop placement methods that can meet the needs of multilingual students, *how* the multilingual students make placement decisions, which is fundamental, needs to be understood before we proceed to improve the placement practices of multilingual students in US college composition programs.

This chapter *reveals* how multilingual students make their placement decisions about first-year composition courses. Specifically, it looks closely at various sources of placement information exploited by the focal multilingual students when they chose a first-year writing course. Building on a discussion of different sources of placement information, I consider that these sources are key conditions that make student agency in placement decisions possible. Chapter 2 is the central part of the book; it leads to a discussion of how the multilingual students exercise agency in their placement decisions in chapters 3–5 and a close examination of academic advising and its role in students' placement decisions in chapter 6.

DOI: 10.7330/9781607325482.c002

HOW MULTILINGUAL WRITERS MAKE
PLACEMENT DECISIONS

A series of my four in-depth interviews with the 11 multilingual writers has generated an understanding of how the students made their placement decisions. Specifically, there were particular sources of placement information that influenced the ways the multilingual students chose to take a mainstream or multilingual composition course (see appendix C). These sources of placement information were as follows:

- academic advisors' recommendations
- other students' past experiences in taking first-year composition courses
- new student orientation
- other sources that provide placement-related information

In what follows, I discuss how the focal multilingual students managed to obtain placement information from these sources and subsequently exploited them when they made their placement decisions.

Academic Advisors' Recommendations

The focal multilingual students primarily relied on recommendations from their academic advisors when they decided what writing course they would take. Of the 11 students, six of them made the decision to take a multilingual section of first-year composition based on recommendations from their academic advisors. Jasim, in his first interview in September 2010, said the academic advisor chose ENG 107 for him. According to Jasim, the advisor told him that international students should take ENG 107.

> He [the advisor] did not tell me much, actually. He told me that these writing courses [ENG 107 and ENG 108] are required. He said I have IELTS scores, so I should take ENG 107. He just told me I have to take it. It is required. (Jasim, Interview I)

When I asked Jasim whether his academic advisor explained to him about available placement options in the writing program, Jasim gave me a surprised look and asked me back, "Really? I did not know that I have options. I thought it was fixed. ENG 101 and ENG 102 are for people from the United States, ENG 107 and ENG 108 are for international students." He continued, raising three questions: "Actually, what is the difference between ENG 101 and ENG 107? Why do you guys separate classes for international students? Do you guys use the same books?" This shows that Jasim was concerned about his English courses and wanted to find out more about them. At the same time, it demonstrated that he did not receive complete information about first-year composition placement from his academic advisor. It is also worth noting that the information about ENG 107 Jasim had received was inaccurate. In fact, as described in chapter 1 under the research context, international multilingual students' placement options are not limited to multilingual composition sections; they have an option to take a mainstream composition section if they wish to.

Like Jasim, Pascal chose to take a multilingual section of first-year composition based on his academic advisor's recommendations. Pascal registered for classes online, including ENG 107, while he was in Amsterdam, Netherlands. Pascal did not meet with his academic advisor but corresponded with him through email. Pascal said he took ENG 107 based on the academic advisor's email message in which he was told: "'You should take ENG 107 and ENG 108.' So, I decided to take it [ENG 107] from what he told me." Pascal added that his academic advisor did not give him any other explanations why it had to be these two courses. Pascal mentioned that he really did not know other options of first-year writing classes. "I just knew the class I am taking."

Mei, Chan, and Joel also decided to take ENG 107 based on recommendations from their academic advisors. Mei said: "My academic advisor gave me suggestions to enroll in this class [ENG 107]."[1] Like Mei, Chan said: " I just followed my advisor. She told me to take ENG 107." Joel also followed his academic advisor's recommendations for taking WAC 107. "She [the academic advisor] told me that I have to take this class [WAC 107], and I am okay [with it]."[2]

Askar was another student who decided to take a multilingual composition section based on recommendations from his academic advisor. He recalled the time when he had a meeting with his academic advisor:

> My advisor told me that since my [iBT] TOEFL score [96] was good, I have two choices [ENG 101 or ENG 107]. I thought ENG 101 is too hard for me and it is for native speakers. I did not want to put extra work on myself. My advisor told me that ENG 107 is way easier. So I just chose ENG 107. It is my own decision. (Askar, Interview I)

Even though Askar was the one who made the decisions about the course he wanted to take, he consulted his academic advisor about first-year English courses and received complete information, which he could use when he enrolled in ENG 107—the course that he thought was appropriate for him.

Other Students' Past Experiences in Taking
First-Year Composition Courses
Some of the multilingual students sought out more information about placement from other students who previously took first-year composition courses. Mei, for example, said she knew she had to take ENG 107 from her Chinese friends who previously completed the class. Chan received some information about TOEFL scores and English placement from her Chinese friends who took WAC 107 before. According to her friends, Chan's iBT TOEFL score of 90 would allow her to enroll in ENG 107. Ting knew about WAC 101, WAC 107, ENG 101, ENG 102, ENG 107, and ENG 108 from a friend who went to a high school in China with her. She recalled: "I got all the information about [first-year] English [writing] classes from my friend." Ting also learned more about placement from this friend's experience in taking both mainstream and multilingual composition sections. Ting referred to the placement story of Joyce (pseudonym). Joyce, after graduating from a high school in China, spent another year in a US high school prior to coming to ASU. Since Joyce graduated from a US high school, her academic advisor recommended that she

take ENG 101. However, Joyce did not think she belonged in mainstream composition, so she decided to switch from ENG 101 to ENG 107. Joyce was happier with her own placement decisions. According to Ting, Joyce, based on this placement experience, told Ting that her advisor "cheated and lied" to her. Similar to Ting, Afia knew about English composition placement from other students' past experiences in taking first-year composition. Afia, while explaining her first-semester placement decisions to me, said she knew about English composition placement from her brother and cousin who recently graduated ASU. She recalled: "My brother helped me a lot because he already graduated. He knows that ENG 101 is for native [English] speakers and ENG 107 is much easier because it is for international students." What Afia was told about ENG 101 and ENG 107 is another example that shows placement information has been distributed to multilingual students inaccurately. Afia's brother understood that ENG 101 was for native English-speaking students and ENG 107 was for international students. As I discussed in chapter 1, multilingual students in the ASU writing program have an option to take either a mainstream or multilingual composition section.

New Student Orientation

Another source of placement information that the multilingual students, particularly resident multilingual students, relied on was new student orientation. New student orientation, as discussed by scholars in the field of academic advising, serves "the purpose of informing students about the curriculum, assisting them in planning a first-semester schedule, and introducing the basics of the registration system" (King 2011, 283). The essential goals of new student orientation include the following: "familiarizing students with academic requirements and helping them make realistic assessments of their ability to meet them" (Gordon 1992, 64, quoted in Perigo and Upcraft 1989).

Marco, a resident multilingual student, said he attended new student orientation, where he also registered for classes, including first-year composition. I asked him what happened during his orientation session, and he described what went on in a small group meeting with academic advisors:

> It was a group of about 15 students in the classroom and we all gathered up with, and there were about 4 advisors there. They just told us about what classes were available and what time and gave us a sheet for enrollment. And we just signed up for class[es] through that. It was not like one-on-one experience. (Marco, Interview IV)

I further asked Marco whether the academic advisors specifically informed students about first-year composition courses. Marco replied: "No, not really. They just told us 'ENG 101 and ENG 102 for English courses, if you have not taken them from high school, sign up for those.' Pretty much it." Based on the information he received at new student orientation, Marco did not know that there were different options of first-year writing courses for him to choose from. He said: "The advisors did not go into detail about English classes; they just said 'here is your requirement, you need to take this in your first year.'"

When Marco[3] learned from me that the writing program made different placement options available to students, and, in fact, students were allowed to choose a first-year writing course they wanted to take, he said as follows:

> As a student, I want to know what options I have. I think it would be nice if at the orientation, they [advisors] would let people know what options are for first-year writing classes. It would be also helpful if they can tell us about test score information and placement procedures. (Marco, Interview IV)

In the end, however, Marco enrolled in ENG 101 because "it is generally known [since in high school] it was required. It was not really information about the school [the university] gives me, it is the information I know." Marco said it was his own decision to retake ENG 101, even though he could "jump" into ENG 102 because he already took ENG 101 in his senior year in high school and he earned three credits for that. Marco explained why he decided to retake ENG 101:

I could have gone to ENG 102 this semester [Fall 2010]. It is pretty much my decision to go over it again. I figure I can use it as a reminder of how to get that basic writing processed, instead of just skipping it and not knowing what to do in English classes and the next steps. I thought it will [would] be pretty helpful, so I just enrolled in it. (Marco, Interview I)

Like Marco, Ana, also a resident multilingual student, registered for classes at new student orientation. She explained as follows: "I chose the class [ENG 101] based on my schedule and when I wanted it. I just did whatever day I could go." For Ana, English is like math. "They are just basic; they are required. For English, it is like pick one." When asked whether she knew of other options of first-year composition classes made available to students, she replied: "I just know that I have to take ENG 101 and ENG 102. I do not know other options." Ana continued, "If I had known [about ENG 107 and ENG 108], I might have taken those classes."[4] Ana seemed to be interested in the multilingual composition courses and thought she might benefit from them. One possible reason was because she considered herself to be bilingual who grew up speaking both Spanish and English. Ana remarked: "For bilingual people, they should have more options because their writing is different." Due to her lack of placement option information, Ana said information about different classes should be communicated to incoming students during new student orientation.

I further asked Ana whether she was informed about the Accuplacer Test at new student orientation. Ana said she had no idea about the test and did not know that she could use a score from the test for her English placement. In addition, Ana was not aware that with her ACT English score of 26, she could enroll in ENG 105 (Advanced Composition). Ana lacked awareness of the Accuplacer Test and test score cutoff points; this was mainly because she was not informed and/or advised at new student orientation. Ana's case suggests that not all students necessarily receive complete and accurate placement information at new student orientation. It is also possible that academic advisors at new student orientation did not recommend ENG

105 to Ana because her ACT score was borderline and/or the academic advisors themselves might not be aware of test score ranges and course placement.

Other Sources Providing Placement-Related Information

The focal multilingual students did not rely on only one source of information when they chose to enroll in their first-semester writing course. They looked into other sources that provided placement-related information, such as online freshman orientation, an online class search, a major map and DARS. In DARS, a list of requirement courses is included, and students can keep track of which requirements are satisfied and which requirements remain to be fulfilled. In the major map, there is a list of courses recommended for each semester; first-year composition courses are listed in the first two semesters. Mei and Chan, for instance, tried to find more information about first-year composition from these sources and they found them very helpful. Like Mei and Chan, Ana said she primarily relied on information about required courses on her major map and DARS. Jonas learned about first-year composition placement information by searching the university's various websites and looking it up from his major map. This student learned about English placement before consulting his academic advisor. Here Jonas recalled: "I had to find everything on the Internet. I did not know about advising. I found out about the classes by myself before I spoke with my academic advisor."

To recapitulate, the focal multilingual students made their placement decisions by exploiting the information they managed to obtain from various sources of placement. Yet, they did not necessarily receive accurate and complete information about English course placement from some sources, such as academic advisors, new student orientation, and other students' past experiences in taking first-year composition. Among the four sources of placement information, recommendations from academic advisors, both one-on-one advising and group advising at new student orientation, were apparently the most influential factors that determined students' placement decisions. At the same time, recommendations from academic advisors seemed to be the worse source compared to the other two sources in terms of the quality of the information. The multilingual students were partially informed about available placement options by their academic advisors and from new student orientation. For instance, the multilingual students were informed that mainstream composition sections were for native English-speaking students only and multilingual composition sections were for international students.

SOURCES OF PLACEMENT INFORMATION: KEY CONDITIONS FOR AGENCY

Using placement information from different sources: academic advisors' recommendations, other students' past experiences in taking first-year composition courses, new student orientation, and other sources that provided placement-related information, the focal multilingual students were able to make their placement decisions about first-year composition courses. I consider these sources of placement information to be important conditions that make student agency in placement decisions possible. Agency, as I delineated in chapter 1, is the capacity to act or not to act contingent upon various conditions. My theory of agency[5] was also grounded on existing definitions of agency developed by scholars in related fields including, anthropology (e.g., Ahearn 2001), rhetoric (e.g., Callinicos 1988; Flannery 1991; Hauser 2004; Young 2008), and applied linguistics (e.g., van Lier 2009). In addition to such key conditions, there is another essential condition that makes student agency in placement decisions possible, which is freedom to choose writing courses that the studied writing program gave to students (see chapter 1). In short, conditions that make student agency in placement decisions possible include different sources of placement information and the freedom to choose writing courses.

With the theory of agency I developed, I propose that when conditions for agency are appropriate and/or optimal, multilingual students are able to *negotiate* their placement, choose to *accept* or *deny* their original placement, *self-assess* their proficiency level when they choose a writing course, *question* their placement, and *plan* for placement. I call these capacities "*acts of agency*."[6] These acts of agency, which are complex, take place when the multilingual students make their placement decisions. I will explicate these acts of agency through the placement stories of Afia, Joel, Jonas, Pascal, Jasim, Chan, and Ting in the next three theme-based chapters.

CHAPTER REFLECTION

This chapter lays the foundation for rest of the book, especially chapters 3–6 and 8. It first provides a better understanding of *how* the focal multilingual students made their first-year composition placement decisions by exploiting different sources of placement information. Each source of placement influenced the way the focal multilingual students chose their first-year writing courses. Important and useful information about how placement decisions are scrutinized in this chapter is an essential springboard for a discussion of how the focal multilingual students exercised agency in their placement decisions (chapters 3–5), a discussion of the role of academic advising/advisors in the placement of multilingual students into first-year composition courses (chapter 6), and a discussion of how student agency can inform the overall programmatic placement of multilingual students in college composition programs (chapter 8) and ways in which writing programs can improve and foster conditions for agency so that student agency is maximized.

NOTES

1.   I conducted the first two interviews with Mei on the same date. The time that this student decided to participate in my research was two months late, and I had already finished the first interviews with other student participants. The first interview had been scheduled between September and October 2010.

2.   Like Mei's case, the time that Joel participated in the study was two months late.

3.   Marco learned about first-year composition placement options during our interviews; I acknowledged that this affected Marco's responses and the study.

4.   Like Marco, Ana learned about these placement options during our interviews; and I acknowledged that this affected Ana's responses and the study.

5.   See chapter 1 (under the section Agency: A Theoretical Framework) and appendix C for a detailed discussion of how I developed my theory of agency.

6.   See appendix C for a detailed description of and reflection on how I developed the acts of agency.

3
NEGOTIATING PLACEMENT VS. ACCEPTING PLACEMENT

I told my academic advisor that I did not want to waste time in WAC 107 and I am a transfer student. So, I asked "should I take WAC 107?"

—Afia

. . . For me, it [WAC 107] is my dessert.

—Joel

The placement experiences of Afia and Joel discussed in this chapter demonstrate why and how the students chose to negotiate and accept their placement. Based on their standardized test scores, the two resident multilingual students were placed into WAC 107 (a developmental writing course). While Afia chose not to accept her original placement and negotiated it in order to be able to take ENG 107, Joel found it fine to be enrolled in this developmental writing course. To showcase their entire placement decision processes, I also consider what went into their placement experiences and what came after the placement decisions were made. Building on these two placement cases, the chapter argues that the more placement information is made available to students the more students are able to exercise agency in their placement decisions.

BACKGROUND
Afia. Originally from Qatar, Afia permanently moved to the United States in July 2009 to live with her brother who already settled down in the country. Their parents planned to migrate

DOI: 10.7330/9781607325482.c003

to the States after their retirement. Afia was already in her junior year when she transferred from a university in her home country to ASU, where she majored in computer information systems. Afia completed first-year writing courses at her previous institution, but she was not able to transfer credits to the current institution, so she had to repeat them. Afia first learned about options of freshman composition from her brother and cousin who graduated from ASU. They told Afia that ENG 101 was for native English speaking students, and ENG 107 was for international students. According to Afia, her brother told her as follows: "ENG 107 is much easier because it is for international students." Afia also learned from a major map that she would have to take ENG 108 after completing ENG 107. This information was confirmed when Afia met with her academic advisor, who recommended that she should take ENG 107 and ENG 108. Afia's academic advisor also informed her that she could take ENG 101 if she wanted. Afia, however, preferred the multilingual composition track because "I think ENG 107 is much easier than ENG 101."

Joel. Also a transfer student, Joel[1] was originally from Mexico, where he had one year left to finish his bachelor's degree in international relations from a technological college. He was married to an American and had US resident status. He had already been in the Southwest for three years when this research began. At the current institution, Joel majored in political science. While working on his degree in the United States, he also worked for an immigration law firm helping clients who were Spanish speakers on immigration issues. Like Afia, Joel completed required writing courses at his previous institution but was not able to transfer the credits and had to repeat the first-year writing sequence at the new institution. The one and only source of placement information Joel relied on was his academic advisor. Joel recalled what he learned from his academic advisor. "I know they [the writing program] use TOEFL scores, and from there they decide where to place us depending on our scores," he said. According to Joel, his academic advisor also told him that he had to finish ENG 107 before he could take ENG 108.

"I DID NOT WANT TO WASTE TIME IN WAC 107": NEGOTIATING PLACEMENT OPTIONS

Afia's case is an example of how obtaining sufficient placement information can allow students to exercise agency in their placement decisions, particularly negotiating placement options. Afia would not have been able to take ENG 107 if her academic advisor had not informed her about the Accuplacer Test. Afia was originally enrolled in WAC 107 due to her iBT TOEFL score (74 out of 120). When Afia and I first met, Afia shared with me what went on during her placement decision process: "First, they [the writing program] put me in WAC 107 because my TOEFL score. I got 74. They tell me I should get 83 or above to get in ENG 107." Right after visiting the writing program office, Afia met with her academic advisor to discuss her placement. Afia informed her academic advisor that she should not take WAC 107, reasoning that she was a transfer student and had previously completed first-year writing courses. Afia recalled a conversation with her academic advisor: "I told my academic advisor that I did not want to waste time in WAC 107 and I am a transfer student. So, I asked 'should I take WAC 107?'"

When the academic advisor learned about Afia's situation, she informed Afia about the Accuplacer Test, a placement test for a first-year English course administered by the University Testing and Scanning Services. Students have an option to take this placement test if they do not have test scores or are not satisfied with their test scores. According to Afia, her academic advisor recommended that she take the test. "My advisor told me to take this chance and try my best for this written test. She said if I get a score of 5, I could enroll in ENG 107," said Afia. After meeting with her academic advisor, Afia decided to take the Accuplacer Test on the first week of Fall 2010. Fortunately, she received a score of 5, which was a minimum cutoff point to be placed into ENG 107. Afia said she spent about 40 minutes (one hour is allowed) to complete a five hundred–word essay. "It was easy. It's more opinion based," Afia added. "When I printed my essay, I know a score right away. Then, a lady told me 'congratulations, you can register for ENG 107,'" Afia described what she experienced on the day she took the test. Apparently, Afia liked the Accuplacer Test because "I did not have to take three English classes." She had to only take the regular first-year writing sequence, no WAC 107 as an additional class. Afia decided to drop WAC 107 and registered for ENG 107 during the first week of the semester. Afia missed the first day of classes, so she went to discuss her situation with her ENG 107 instructor. "I told her that I took the Accuplacer Test, and I switched from WAC 107 to ENG 107." The instructor understood Afia's situation, since this was not new to her as well as other instructors of multilingual students in this writing program. It was one of the writing program's placement policies that allowed multilingual students to switch sections up to two weeks after the semester began.

After Placement Decisions Were Made

I was also interested in learning how Afia felt after her first-semester placement decision was made. I asked Afia to talk about her experience in her ENG 107 class. Our conversation took place in September 2010, which was about a month after Fall 2010 had started. Afia was very straightforward:

> At the beginning, I really don't like ENG 107 because I already took ENG 101 and ENG 102 in my country. I thought it's like wasting time. But I feel like Thank God I am taking it. It helps me a lot. It improves my writing and speaking. Now everything is cool. We are improving our writing by reviewing each other's papers. I know how to organize my writing, and I write more professionally. It's good. (Afia, Interview I)

Afia was happy with her placement into ENG 107 and did fine enough in the class; she earned a B for the final course grade. She expressed how the class fit her English proficiency level:

> I think it is the most effective class for me. I like this class because most of the students are not native English Americans. They are like me, so they speak like me, I don't feel shy when I speak to them, and I make a lot of friends. That is why I prefer ENG 107 rather than taking ENG 101. Unlike in other classes, I tend to

be very quiet. I feel like everyone is hearing me and looking to my accent. So the English class is where I talk the most. (Afia, Interview II)

What Afia felt about being in a class with students who were *like* her echoes what was found in Costino and Hyon's (2007) study, which suggested that students of varying residency statuses (US-born, US-resident immigrant, and international) preferred either mainstream or multilingual composition because each class had students who were like them. As pointed out by Costino and Hyon, their student participants "sought a class with students who reflected some aspects of themselves" (76), and these aspects included "English proficiency level . . . international residency status, multilingual experience, or national origin" (76).

Afia also noted that taking an English class with non-native English speakers came with some disadvantages, especially where "we can't teach each other when it comes to speaking. We are all weak." Nonetheless, she still preferred an English class with non-native speaking counterparts. One main reason, as Afia explained, for her preference had to do with the way her instructor worked with students in the class. "The teacher is very considerate. She realizes that students are not Americans. So she speaks slowly. She tries to explain everything. I like her a lot. When she asks questions, I respond to her. I usually go to her office to ask her about my writing."

When Afia was in the process of registration for classes for Spring 2011, she went to see her academic advisor to seek consultation about classes in computer information systems, which was her major. However, Afia said she did not need any advice on a second-semester English writing course. She explained as follows: "I tried to leave ENG 108 to the end because I thought that my English will have already improved by the time I take it. So I thought I would not take it [in Spring 2011]. But most of my courses need ENG 108 [as a prerequisite], including ENG 302 [Business writing]." In the end, Afia decided to register for ENG 108 for Spring 2011. Here she recalled: "Without asking my advisor, I enroll in ENG 108 because I need to take it. It's my own decision. I know that ENG 108 will be about writing, so it will help improve my writing."

About a month after Spring 2011 had started, Afia and I met for our third interview in February. The first thing Afia mentioned to me was that: "ENG 108 is a lot more difficult than ENG 107." She then mentioned her first writing assignment's grade, which she learned about the day before our interview:

> I should work hard, a lot harder, you know. I am getting worried. I get shocked when I get my grade. I got really bad score on the first assignment. It's an E. But if I work on revision, I can get a D. This class is not like ENG 107 where I just submitted a paper and I ended up with a B and I am satisfied with it because I hate writing. I thought ENG 108 is gonna be like ENG 107. (Afia, Interview III)

In this first writing assignment, Afia and her fellow classmates were required to write about a controversial issue. She chose to examine a topic of education in her country, particularly focusing on an ongoing debate concerning boys and girls studying in the same classroom. According to Afia, the instructor liked her topic, but she had a concern about some grammatical problems and sentence level issues in her writing.

When we met for the last interview, I asked Afia to reflect on her overall experiences with first-year composition placement. Afia told me that even though she was happy with her decisions to take the multilingual track of first-year composition, especially the ENG 107 class, she regretted that she did not take WAC 107:

> If I came to ASU for my freshman year, I would take WAC 107. I think it helps. I found the problem, you know. If we move first to ENG 107, it is kind of falling. If I took WAC 107, I would be more prepared and aware of those [writing] skills. That's why I got a B in ENG 107 and I don't know what I am going to get in ENG 108. (Afia, Interview IV)

She then referred back to the Accuplacer Test she took early in the fall semester, elaborating that a score of 5 (out of 8) did not mean that she would be successful. Afia explained:

> Even though I got 5 on the Accuplacer Test, you know when I got in ENG 107 is totally different. Maybe in the placement test, they look at how many words I can write. It's no time to grade. It's so fast. Whenever you finish, you get the score. I think they count the words. It's not a good measure for your writing skills. I am so worried about my ENG 108. (Afia, Interview IV)

It is clear that what Afia felt about the Accuplacer Test in this last interview conducted in April 2011 was totally different from her feelings about the test in the first interview carried out in September 2010. Based on her experience with the Accuplacer Test, Afia recommended that incoming international multilingual students take WAC 107 to help prepare them for ENG 107 and ENG 108:

> WAC 107 will help them a lot. When they take ENG 107, they will be more prepared. I wanted to tell students who take WAC 107 not to think it's a waste of time. After that, they will get benefit from the class. They will discover that they need it because it's not easy in ENG 107. There are certain requirements and some skills that we can develop in WAC 107. (Afia, Interview IV)

As discussed earlier, Afia seemed to struggle in ENG 108. However, she learned a lot from taking the class. She had a lot to say about it:

> I think I improve a lot in ENG 108. It's more difficult than ENG 107. I don't like writing, but now it's easier to write than before. In the past, I did not know how to express my ideas in English. I think something and I wrote different things. Now I am getting used to. I feel like it's easier for me. At first, it was hard. Now it's okay. (Afia, Interview IV)

Afia went on to elaborate that "I write faster than before. It usually took like 3 hours. Now it takes me about 1.5 hours to finish writing a paper. I spent less time. I think I know how to deliver my message." While at the beginning of Spring 2011 semester, Afia was very concerned about her grades and performance in ENG 108. When she was getting close to the end of the semester, she was more relaxed and did not think that these grade things were essential anymore:

I might end up with a B in ENG 108. But the more importance is what I learn. Grades do not really matter. For me, a B is okay. And I would like to have more talking in the class. I know how to write, but I need to speak with people. More discussions and presentations in the class would be great. (Afia, Interview IV)

Afia said she remembered that her ENG 108 instructor told her and fellow classmates to "just keep writing," and "even though we are international students, we can write as good as native speakers."

Based on her first-year composition placement experience, Afia concluded, "I made the right decisions to take ENG 107 and ENG 108. Most of my other courses required me to write papers. So, it helps me a lot." As she had been through the first-year composition placement, Afia had one recommendation for the writing program in order to improve the placement of students into first-year writing courses. She would like to see the writing program provide incoming students with information about first-year writing courses, such as what each course was about and what types of assignments students would be required to complete would help students have a clear idea of first-year composition.

" . . . FOR ME, IT [WAC 107] IS MY DESSERT": A REASON FOR ACCEPTING PLACEMENT

While Afia chose to negotiate her placement with her academic advisor, Joel preferred to accept his WAC 107 placement. A senior majoring in political science, Joel received all information about placement, including test score cutoffs, available placement options, and placement procedures from his academic advisor. Joel said he followed his academic advisor's recommendations for taking WAC 107. "She told me that I have to take this class, and I am okay." Joel recalled the time when he met with his academic advisor:

According to my advisor, I have this score [542 out of 677, Paper-based Test TOEFL], so I have to take WAC 107, and I do not have complaints about it. Well, I will see in this way . . . We have to be in the class because we have to be. 'From that score, we have this class for you,' even though I think I am better than that. (Joel, Interview I)

Even though he was willing to take WAC 107, Joel noted that, "with my level, I don't think I will have to take WAC 107. I feel more confident and comfortable with the writing. But, yeah, I'm not saying that I speak perfect English and I write perfectly."

However, Joel explained that because he was going to graduate in Spring 2012, "it does not matter if I advance in ENG 108 or else; it is gonna be the same time. So, it is okay. If I have to take it, I gonna take it." For Joel, taking WAC 107 was like having a "dessert" because he thought the class was not too difficult compared to other higher-level courses; and he could write whatever he wanted:

> The way I see this class for me is a dessert. Why? I am not that stressed. I type and I talk about whatever I want to. I do not think that is pressure. Well, because, for example, other higher-level courses like philosophy and politics in which I had to put a lot of attention. I write about the topic that I want in the English class. I just type it. It is more easy. I do not feel that pressure. For me, it is my dessert. (Joel, Interview II)

After Placement Decisions Were Made

After he completed WAC 107 with a grade of A in Spring 2010, Joel was subsequently enrolled in ENG 107 in Fall 2010; his placement decision was based on recommendations from his academic advisor. Even though Joel did not have any complaints about his placement into ENG 107 and seemed to be happy with this decision, he did not really enjoy the class and had negative impressions of his classmates. Joel elaborated:

> The class could be better if we [were] more fluent and participated more, but they [most of students] do not want to participate in class activities. The interaction in class is too slow and almost nothing. There is nothing. They are so quiet and reserved. No one says anything. They just smile. I have to raise

my hand and say something. Sometimes it is kind of frustrating. (Joel, Interview I)

In Joel's view, his classmates "are still thinking they are in high schools." Joel, in his early thirties, went on to explain that his classmates' topic selection for controversial topics was "really for high school or elementary level like global warming, immigration, and gay marriage." That is why "I don't like the topics they picked. They don't make any sense. They don't understand the points. I don't like the level of students," Joel expressed.

When asked whether there were things that he liked about the class, Joel said that even though the class "is terrible," he had freedom to write about topics he liked and that made him feel comfortable. "I wrote a paper about anarchy and nobody in my class understood it, except the instructor. No one had questions," Joel explained. However, Joel found that his classmates' writing skills "are good" when "I reviewed their essays." He came to his own conclusion that the main reason his classmates "tended not to speak in class was because they may be afraid of their accent." He then noted: "I do have an accent, too."

Even though Joel knew he would be taking ENG 108 in Spring 2011, he managed to meet with his academic advisor to discuss his second-semester writing course. Since he knew he had to take the course, Joel noted as follows: "It's not my decision. It's not just I decide to do it. I have to do, and I have to be in ENG 108." When I met Joel for our third interview in February 2011, I asked him how his ENG 108 class was going. "Everything is fine," Joel replied and went on to say as follows:

> We are working on an argumentative paper. We are doing more research. I think this is different from ENG 107. Besides that, I think it's the same. The lack of participation in class is still the same. Students are quiet in the class . . . the same situation like last semester. Sometimes it makes the class very slow and boring . . . I am the one who participates in the class. I think this also shows our respect [to the instructor]. You are there to learn. I feel really awkward if I don't say anything. (Joel, Interview III)

In one class activity, Joel continued, students were supposed to bring their rough drafts for peer review. He brought his, but none of his group members did, and "this making the class really boring. It goes slowly. So I had to read my paper by myself again. We should be more professional than this. We are not elementary school students. We are now in college. You are here because you want to be here."

Even though his overall first-year composition experiences, especially in ENG 107 and ENG 108, were not pleasant, Joel was satisfied with his decisions to take three writing classes, starting from WAC 107, ENG 107, and ENG 108. He revealed: "I am very satisfied. I don't have any complaints. For me, it's like I do what I have to do, and I took advantage from that. In that way, I am happy. It's something that will help me to finish my degree. That way, I am completely satisfied. Especially my age, I am not 18 years old."

In completing the first-year composition sequence, Joel was happy with his English skills. "My English now is better," he said. To prove this, Joel asked me to listen to his interview recordings and see how much he had improved over the course of one academic year. Here is what he said to me: "You can check your audio recordings. The way I structure my ideas and sentences. I make more sense. I can see myself improve. I know how to structure my essays. I feel more comfortable with my English. What I learned in English classes helped me in writing papers in other classes."

Based on his experiences with first-year composition placement, Joel recommended that incoming international students, who did not feel comfortable with their TOEFL scores, take the Accuplacer Test. "They [the writing program] give an option [an opportunity to take the test]. Then your academic advisor will help you with your placement decisions."

CHAPTER REFLECTION

Negotiating and accepting placement were the two acts of agency highlighted in this chapter. While Afia negotiated placement options, Joel chose to accept his placement into WAC 107. The two multilingual students were able to exercise agency in their placement decision processes because of sufficient and necessary information they received from their academic advisors and from other students' past experiences in taking first-year composition courses, especially in the case of Afia. Prior to meeting with her academic advisor, Afia received some information about placement options from her brother and cousin who previously took first-year writing courses at ASU. When meeting with her academic advisor, she negotiated placement options, inquiring whether she should take ENG 107, instead of WAC 107. When the academic advisor informed her about the Accuplacer Test, Afia did not hesitate to take this written placement test right away. In the end, she was able to take ENG 107 as she wanted. Joel, on the contrary, was fine with his original placement into WAC 107, even though he thought his proficiency could allow him to take ENG 107. He did not even ask his academic advisor if he could skip WAC 107 and go straight to ENG 107.

What followed their placement decisions was also worth a close examination. While Afia kind of regretted that she skipped WAC 107, Joel, in fact, did not seem to like both the WAC 107 and ENG 107 classes. In the case of Afia, she lacked some writing skills required of being successful in ENG 107. Thus, she admitted that taking WAC 107 would help better prepare her for the writing assigned in ENG 107. Joel did not have pleasant experiences in or great impressions of either WAC 107 and ENG 107. Both the classes and his classmates bored him. This could possibly be explained because his level of English proficiency was ahead of his classmates, who were 18 years old and recently graduated from high schools. Joel, in his early thirties, had experience with English writing before; he was also working as an attorney assistant while completing his political science degree at this institution.

The cases of Afia and Joel, especially when they were dissatisfied with their placement, resulted from their lack of necessary information about what is taught in each first-year writing course option. Specifically, they did not have a clear sense of what WAC 107 and ENG 107 were about. To mitigate this lack-of-necessary placement information and/or to prevent this similar situation at other institutions, writing programs should provide incoming students with information about available options of first-year writing courses, the differences among those options, what students will be doing in each course, and details about assignments they will be asked to complete. These pieces of information are essential, and students need them, especially when they choose which first-year writing course is right for them.

NOTE

1.   I conducted the first two interviews with Joel on the same day in November 2010. The time that this student decided to participate in the study was late, and I had already finished the first interviews with other student participants. The first interview had been scheduled between September and October 2010.

4

WHY SELF-ASSESSING IS CRUCIAL FOR PLACEMENT

I have spoken and written a lot of English before. So English was not new to me. I think my level was ENG 107.

—Jonas

ENG 107 is really a beginner class. . . . It is too easy. We have to write essays about ourselves and stuff like that. I don't want to do that anymore, you know since they are like what I used to do in my ESL classes. I get tiring of writing about myself and personal experiences. Ah, I did that for three years now. I am not ESL anymore.

—Pascal

The experiences with first-year composition placement of Jonas and Pascal discussed in this chapter delineate the essentials of self-assessing in placement decisions. The two international multilingual students exercised their agency by self-assessing while they were in the process of choosing first-year writing courses that they thought were right for them. Both Jonas and Pascal were not satisfied with their original placement into WAC 107 and ENG 107, respectively; this was one thing they had in common. What made these two cases different? Jonas tried every possible way to make his placement into ENG 107 possible. Unlike Jonas, Pascal self-assessed but did not take action. He ended up taking multilingual composition courses (ENG 107 and ENG 108), even though he contended that his English proficiency was beyond ESL. The two placement cases, especially the case of Pascal, raises an important concern about how to design the first-year L2 writing curriculum that would best address the abilities, needs, and identities of multilingual

DOI: 10.7330/9781607325482.c004

students whose educational and proficiency backgrounds are increasingly diverse (Costino and Hyon 2007).

BACKGROUND

Jonas. Jonas[1] was originally from Oslo, Norway. He majored in business administration before switching to political science. His iBT TOEFEL score of 77 placed him into WAC 107, and he learned about this placement when he was still in his country. Jonas said he was not aware of academic advising, and that he did not consult anyone about English course placement. "I knew nothing about academic advising," he recalled. Jonas said he found out about placement information, including placement procedures, placement options, and score requirements, from the university's websites. Jonas's understanding about English placement was as follows: "There is one class below ENG 107, but I'm not sure if we can take a class above ENG 107 in the first semester. I know if I get a C or better in ENG 107, I can go to ENG 108." When he found out about the Accuplacer Test, he took the test and scored 5 out of 8 on the WritePlacer section; and finally he was able to take ENG 107 as he wanted.

Pascal. Pascal, a freshman originally from France, majored in economics. While French is his first language, Pascal is able to speak four other languages, including German, English, Arabic, and Japanese. He was born in France then moved to Morocco where he picked up Arabic; to Vienna where he learned German and English; and ended up living in Amsterdam before coming to the United States. Pascal was in ESL classes in a high school in Vienna when he first learned English five years ago. At that time, he did not know how to speak English at all.

His iBT TOEFL score of 102 placed him into ENG 107. Pascal said he learned from his academic advisor that ENG 107 and ENG 108 were first-year writing courses for international students. According to Pascal, the academic advisor also informed him that if he did not want to put extra work on writing courses, the multilingual composition track could be a better option. Pascal mentioned that he did not know about other first-year composition course options and did not understand how each option was different from one another. "I just knew the class I'm taking," Pascal said. He also noted that his first semester's registration and course selection "was a bit confusing." Pascal said he took the classes from what the academic advisor told him.

SELF-ASSESSING FOR A BETTER PLACEMENT OPTION

Jonas told me that he was quite disappointed when he first learned that he was placed into WAC 107. Here he explained: "I have spoken and written a lot of English before. So English was not new to me. I think my level was ENG 107." This was where things started. When Jonas first arrived to the university, the first thing he did was to find out more about first-year English course placement. He recalled: "I called a lot of people and looked down the web page and searched on the Internet on the university's websites [again]." His effort paid off. Jonas learned about the Accuplacer Test and managed to enroll in ENG 107, the writing course that he thought was right for him. Jonas recalled:

> I did the placement test and got a better score [5 out of 8]. I dropped WAC 107 and enrolled in ENG 107 instead. I think it was a good decision. It is very good to do the Accuplacer Test. I remember I had one hour. I had to write an essay. Something about Abraham Lincoln. 'Abraham said this, and what do you think about this?' I did not know Abraham Lincoln before. I just had topic sentences for each paragraph. (Jonas, Interview I)

Clearly, this suggests the agentiveness of the student. It started from his dissatisfaction with WAC 107 placement. Then Jonas self-assessed his English proficiency while he managed to find out more about first-year composition placement. In the end, the necessary placement information Jonas obtained allowed him to proceed to the first-year writing courses he wanted to take.

As we can tell, Jonas was happy that there were such things like the Accuplacer Test. "The placement test is good," he said. "If I did not know about it, I would have to do WAC 107. I think they [The University Testing and Scanning Service] should do more marketing on this." Jonas's comments suggest that not all incoming undergraduate students know of this written placement test option. One main reason, as I discussed in chapter 6, was that not every academic advisor informed his/her multilingual student advisees about the Accuplacer Test (see chapter 6 for a detailed discussion).

After Placement Decisions Were Made
Jonas had been taking ENG 107 for about a month when we met for our first interview in September 2010. I asked Jonas to share with me his overall impression of the class. "The class is very good. I like the class very much," he replied. "I think I'm in the right class. I'm doing well in ENG 107." Jonas elaborated that the class "helps me improve my English, especially when you come to another country and have to learn English better. If you are good in English, you do better in other classes at college as well." Jonas further commented on different options of first-year composition provided for students:

> I think it's very smart to have a class like that. It's also good to have different levels you can enroll in so you can see the differences. If you are very good in [at] English, you can go on a good level. And if you are poor, you can go to a lower level. I think it's the good system with different levels. (Jonas, Interview I)

When we met for our second interview in November 2010, Jonas talked about what he liked and did not like about ENG 107. He said ENG 107 "is one of my good classes that I have. It's very nice class to go to. I go there to learn about different cultures. Everybody is in the same situation. Nobody speaks English perfectly and fluently as native speakers do. So, everybody had something in common. It's easier to make friends there." More important, Jonas perceived that the class was good for him because "everybody is a foreigner and the teacher knows that and she focuses on content more than grammatical errors." This suggests that Jonas did not perceive that taking a writing class with non-native English speaking students came with disadvantages. "No, I don't think so. It's good to have a class without native speakers as well because you can also have other classes with native speakers as well."

Jonas had already registered for his Spring 2011 courses, including ENG 108, before we met for our second interview. I also learned from Jonas that he decided to switch his major from business administration to supply chain management and finally settled on political science. A major reason for this change was because he could take easier math. Since Jonas switched his major, he was assigned a new academic advisor. This academic advisor informed him to take ENG 108. "He just said that I needed to take ENG 108, so that was a requirement." Jonas was aware that both ENG 107 and ENG 108 were requirements for graduation. "I need to take ENG 107 and ENG 108 in order to graduate. I need to do, but I also think it's smart because I learn how to write better."

Based on his placement experiences, Jonas would like to see the university's undergraduate admissions office send information about first-year composition placement directly to international students. He mentioned this because he was one of the students who did not know much about registration, course offerings, and English course placement, and he had to search for this information on the university's websites on his own while he was in his country.

"WHY ENG 107? I AM NOT ESL"

Like Jonas, Pascal self-assessed his English proficiency while he was in the process of making placement decisions. However, the outcome of their self-assessment was different. Pascal, who scored 102 (out of 120) on the iBT TOEFL, was still enrolled in ENG 107, the course that he claimed to be below his level:

> ENG 107 is really a beginner class. It's too easy. The class is good but the level is too low. We are writing in ESL level. We have to write essays about ourselves and stuff like that. I don't want to do that anymore, you know since they are like what I used to do in my ESL classes. I get tiring of writing about myself and personal experience. Ah, I did that for three years now. I am not ESL

anymore. I could take my own essay I did before and gave it to her [the instructor], you know. (Pascal, Interview I)

Apparently, Pascal thought that his English proficiency was beyond ESL level, so he said, "I should have not been in ENG 107; instead I think I could be in ENG 108 right now." What Pascale said raises two essential concerns. First, it suggested that Pascal was not aware that students in mainstream composition courses also wrote essays about themselves. This also implies that not all incoming students necessarily understand what first-year composition is about and what kind of writing assignments are required. Second, Pascal's placement account does raise questions such as how to best design curricula that would address the abilities, needs, and identities of multilingual students whose educational and proficiency backgrounds are diverse (Costino and Hyon 2007). For example, some types of instruction and assignments that position multilingual students like Pascal as "newcomers or outsiders to U.S. culture" (Harklau 2000; Harklau, Losey, and Siegal 1999; Costino and Hyon, 2007, 78) should be reevaluated.

Throughout my interviews with Pascal, he seemed very contradictory. Here is one example. Even though Pascal said "ENG 107 was not really interesting for me anymore," he liked its "international diversity" in which everyone came from different cultural and language backgrounds. Still, he seemed unhappy with the way his teacher treated him and his classmates:

> In the class where I am right now, it's not frustrating. The teacher is really nice. It's good. But, sometimes, it is annoying because when the teacher talks, you feel like she thinks you are an ESL student, you do not speak English, you know. She uses easy words. We are smarter than that, you know. I think I move beyond that level. I am more than an ESL student compared to average ESL students. My English is not as good as French, but I would say I'm fluent in English. (Pascal, Interview I)

I met Pascal again for our second interview in November 2010. Pascal had already made his decision to take ENG 108 in Spring 2011 before the interview. He shared with me what went on in a meeting with his academic advisor:

> I have registered for ENG 108 because my academic advisor told me. She said it would be better for me to take ENG 108. It's because ENG 102 is harder. Since I am doing more credits next semester, it would be easier for me to have ENG 108 than ENG 102; otherwise I will spend a lot of my time doing English. I have other classes like economics and math, way higher level. I need time for these classes. (Pascal, Interview II)

Apparently, Pascal thought about taking ENG 102 but decided not to do so in the end. His academic advisor, according to Pascal, explained to him that ENG 108 should be better for him; this decision was mainly because he was an international student. Pascal learned from his academic advisor that ENG 108 and ENG 102 were basically the same; the only difference was that while he would be with American students in ENG 102, he would be with international students in ENG 108. Using placement information obtained from his academic advisor, Pascal said he was the one who decided to take ENG 108. He summed up his second-semester English placement decision: "Oh, yeah. It's my own decision. I asked my academic advisor what would be better. But, still you know, I can always say no if I don't want to take this class. So it's still good to stay in the international environment. Well, it's better to be with people from everywhere, you know."

About a month after Spring 2011 had started, Pascal and I met for our third interview. Pascal first let me know that he ended up earning an A- in ENG 107. He said he was satisfied with the final grade. We moved on to discuss his current ENG 108. I asked him how his ENG 108 was going, and Pascal replied with disappointment: "I should have taken ENG 102 (laugh). It's the teacher. We've been in school now for six weeks and we haven't done anything, really. He came to class and tried to pronounce the names of the students. Then the class is over. He's not really good. So, ENG 108 would be better if the teacher would be different." Pascal continued, commenting on his ENG 108 class as follows: "The class is not well structured. Basically, there are two people talking in the class, me and one of my friends. Other students are on computers, Facebooking and doing nothing. When the teacher asked questions, I was the only one answering."

It seemed that Pascal was not happy with his instructor's teaching style and classmates' lack of participation and interaction. However, he felt that he was being challenged in ENG 108. Pascal liked the class, thanks to its content (argumentative writing; topics covered included controversies, debates, and definitions). "I feel like I'm more in an American level," he said. However, Pascal thought that he did not learn anything new from the class. He said as follows: "Right now, I am having fun. It's interesting, but it's not giving me anything. It's not bringing me anything in particular. Basically, what we do is the same thing. We go to classrooms and write papers and we get grades on the papers."

While Pascal seemed resistant to the ESL label and treatment, he still chose to enroll in multilingual composition sections in both Fall 2010 and Spring 2011 semesters. One possible reason was that he was recommended by his academic advisor to take multilingual composition courses because they were designed for international students like him. Another possible reason was that he did not want to put extra work on writing classes. If he chose to take ENG 101 and ENG 102, he had to work harder to keep up with native English-speaking peers.

Pascal was also seen confused with his language identity. As you may have remembered, in the first two interviews, Pascal said he was not an ESL student; his English proficiency was beyond that of average ESL students. Then in his third interview, he considered himself to be an advanced ESL student when he said, "there should be an advanced ESL class like ENG 105 [advanced English composition] for American students. Do not put us in ENG 105; otherwise we will be lost. If I were in ENG 105 in the first semester, full of Americans who perfectly know English, I would feel like where was I right now." Nevertheless, Pascal did not deny that taking first-year writing courses was his learning experience. Still, he noted: "If it was not required, I wouldn't take it. I would rather take economics or physics." Pascal believed that it made sense for some students to have to take first-year writing courses. But, for him, he did not think he needed them. "I don't feel like I do," Pascal emphasized. For Pascal, "English classes are the same things. You learn about the topic, write about the topic, go on and on like that. This is always the same thing, and it's not very interesting for me. The only thing I'm happy about is I'm learning a lot of new vocabulary."

When we met for the last interview in April 2011, I mainly asked Pascal to reflect on his overall first-year English placement experiences. Pascal said that even though at one point he was considering taking ENG 102, he was pretty happy with his decisions to take ENG 107 and ENG 108. He explained that in these two classes, especially in ENG 108, "I got an A without really try. I didn't try. It wasn't that hard because perhaps I was with other ESL students, foreigners."

Based on his English placement experiences, Pascal recommended that incoming students see academic advisors before making placement decisions. However, Pascal emphasized that students should decide on the courses they wanted to take themselves. "Really from my experience, look at your SAT or TOEFL scores and decide by yourself. Make the choice yourself. Choose the better class for yourself," he said. "If students get more than 100 points of TOEFL, just go to ENG 101. It just depends if they are lazy or not. If they wanna work, they would be with Americans. It depends what they wanna do."

In addition, Pascal, like Afia, wanted the writing program to improve course descriptions of first-year writing courses by providing more information about what each class was about, brief details of what students would be doing in class, and a preview of writing assignments. Pascal believed that it would help incoming students if the writing program could provide some sample essays written by past students. Pascal also wished that for multilingual students whose English skills were beyond ESL level: "Perhaps, they [the writing program] should have, for example, 107A for beginners, and 107B for higher level students."

CHAPTER REFLECTION

Self-assessing was the act of agency highlighted in this chapter. The two students self-assessed their English proficiency while they made their placement decisions. The outcomes of their self-assessment were different: Jonas was able to take ENG 107 as he wanted. Pascal was still enrolled in ENG 107 and ENG 108, the classes he thought were below his level. At the very beginning, the two students did not receive adequate placement information. They had to figure out ways to obtain more information, so that they could make well-informed placement decisions. Jonas, right after obtaining all necessary placement information, took the Accuplacer Test and finally was able to enroll in ENG 107. For Pascal, even though he maintained his placement into ENG 107 and ENG 108, he still exercised his agency by not choosing the mainstream composition track. In other words, he accepted his placement into ENG 107 (with some complaints and resistance). To recapitulate, the act of self-assessing would not have been possible if the two students did not receive complete placement information.

Pascal's placement account especially raises an essential concern about curriculum design and instruction for linguistically diverse students enrolled in first-year writing courses. While some international multilingual students, like Pascal for example, are advanced learners, some others may still develop their English language proficiency. Similarly, some resident multilingual students may be very proficient and fluent; some others may have difficulty developing their English language skills. If international and resident multilingual students are placed into the same writing course, what kind of instruction can serve their differing needs? A similar question has also been raised, should international multilingual students and resident multilingual students take mainstream composition? Since students are able to place themselves in either mainstream or multilingual option, one of the most productive ways for WPAs to address those two placement- and curriculum-related questions is to design and develop instruction that "address[es] the *differing* abilities and identities of students" (Costino and Hyon 2007, 78; emphasis mine). Specifically, such curricula must "avoid positioning all multilingual students as newcomers or outsiders to U.S. culture. By the same token, pedagogy in the mainstream sections needs to be sensitive to needs of multilingual students, as diverse as they may be, not assuming an insider or native familiarity with either the English language or U.S. culture" (78).

Another effective way is to train our writing teachers to be able to work with multilingual students who come from different backgrounds. Since US higher education has become linguistically diverse, it is essential that writing teachers can address culturally and linguistically diverse students' language needs. It has become common that mainstream composition classrooms enroll multilingual writers; that is why developing writing teachers' abilities to work with these student populations without singling them out is one of the urgent tasks of WPAs. This can be done in various forms, including inviting L2 writing specialists to organize workshops for writing teachers (this applies to institutions that do not have L2 writing specialists). To prepare writing teachers, graduate programs in rhetoric and composition, applied linguistics, and TESOL, among others, should offer a course in teaching L2 writing and make it a requirement for graduate students.

Finally, what we could also do, if resources allow and are available, is to provide as many placement options as possible for students as suggested by Silva (1994). Having various placement options will help us meet differing needs, abilities, and proficiencies of diverse multilingual students

NOTE

1.   I did not have information about Jonas's age and other related background information; this was because I collected the student participants' demographic information (e.g., age, education, and native language) in the final interview. Jonas did not show up after the first two interviews.

5

PLANNING FOR AND QUESTIONING PLACEMENT (AND OTHER ACTS OF AGENCY)

So I was about this close to apply for ENG 102. I kept thinking about it. Then I talked to some of my international student friends. They said that the university made ENG 108 for foreign students. That means it is good for me, you know.
—Jasim

I am not sure about ENG 108. I still consider. Maybe I will drop it or I will choose another class because I can take ENG 108 in the summer session or in the following fall semester.
—Chan

My paper is not so good. I only got 105 out of 150 for the first assignment. After I revised it, I got 125. I calculated the score and the average and my grade. I think it is not so good for my overall GPA. I will end up getting a B. So I decided to withdraw from the class after I know a grade of my first writing assignment . . . I will choose ENG 108 for next semester.
—Ting

The placement experiences of Jasim, Chan, and Ting discussed in this chapter illustrate planning and questioning as the acts of agency. The three students had one thing in common: they were able to plan for and question placement when they obtained sufficient placement information from different sources, including other students' past experiences in taking first-year writing courses and with their academic advisors. These sources of placement, as I argue throughout the book, are key conditions that make student agency possible. Planning and questioning were specifically evident when these three international

DOI: 10.7330/9781607325482.c005

multilingual students were in the process of choosing a second-semester writing course for their spring semester. The three students asked more questions about the placement options they had, as well advantages and disadvantages of each course option. They also did more planning while deciding whether to register for their second-semester writing course in Spring 2011 or to wait until the following fall semester. These acts of agency occurred mainly because the students had a better understanding of English composition placement and knew how and where to find more information about placement. In other words, they made use of their first-semester placement experiences.

In addition, I observed *emerging conditions* for agency that led to *succeeding acts of agency*. To be more specific, these emerging conditions included changing a major of study and transferring to other schools, which made the students do more planning for and questioning their second-semester placement. When these emerging conditions came into play, the succeeding acts of agency were performed: (thinking about) postponing a second-semester writing course to other semesters and withdrawing from the second-semester writing course when placement was not satisfied.

BACKGROUND

Jasim. An Arabic native, Jasim was originally from Dubai, the United Arab Emirates. When this research was conducted, Jasim had been in the United States for almost two years. After graduating from an English medium high school in Dubai, he came to the United States to attend an intensive English program (IEP) in Seattle for one year and moved to Philadelphia to study in another IEP. At ASU, Jasim started his study with electrical engineering but finally settled on industrial engineering. I discussed in detail in chapter 2 that Jasim's first semester placement decision was basically based on his academic advisor's recommendation: international students should take the multilingual composition track. Jasim did not complain about his academic advisor's placement recommendation for ENG 107, but he thought the class was easier than English classes he previously took in an IEP at another US university. The class "was wonderful and I enjoyed it," he said. However, Jasim wanted more from the class: "I was expecting more reading, more class discussion, more interaction between the teacher and students, and more group work." Jasim emphasized: "I want something more challenging." This might be the primary reason for Jasim to consider taking ENG 102 in Spring 2011. "Maybe next semester I will think about ENG 102," Jasim said. He went on to say that for his first semester at this university, "I did not put all my attention on English courses." To Jasim's understanding, international students could not take mainstream composition, "so that is why I did not do research." Jasim ended up earning an A+ in ENG 107.

Chan. A Chinese native, Chan is a transfer student from China, where she studied at a university for two years. Chan was a freshman when first enrolled at ASU. She majored in business communication but attempted to switch to accounting. Learning about first-year composition placement from her friends, Chan was aware that ENG 107 was especially designed for *foreign* students. She was fine with her placement into ENG 107, and she seemed to like the class, too. "The atmosphere of the class is relaxing. The class is small. We are working on the first assignment and we write a story about ourselves. Very interesting," Chan described. "The class did not put some pressure [on me]. There is nothing that I don't like," she said. When asked about the best part of taking a class with non-native speaking students, Chan replied:

> It makes me less nervous. All of us go abroad for study here so we have same experience. We have many problems in our pronunciation, speaking, and writing skills. I feel we are the same and similar. We are on the same track and it makes me feel less nervous. If I am with all native English speakers, I can't understand them. Their pronunciation is perfect. This will make me not willing to open my mouth. But when I hear my classmates who are international students speak every close to native speakers, this will encourage me to practice more. (Chan, Interview II)

When I met Chan again for our second interview; she was close to completing ENG 107. Chan seemed more confidant and said that her writing skills had improved. She earned an A in ENG 107.

Ting. A native Chinese speaker, Ting attended two intensive English programs for one year prior coming to ASU: the first one in Vancouver and the other at the University of British Columbia. Ting majored in math and statistics. Ting learned about first-year composition placement options from a friend of hers who previously completed the first-year writing courses at this institution. Ting said she chose to take ENG 107 by herself and subsequently informed her academic advisor about her placement. Ting believed that the class was right for her. "It's good, and I can handle it. It's not too hard, and it's not too easy. I can learn something new from working on homework and assignments," she explained. Ting continued to say that because she wanted to get an A, she had motivation and was willing to do homework. "I try my best," Ting said. However, she found English classes onerous and admitted that she preferred to spend more time on other classes. "I hate writing papers. I just want to pass it as soon as possible. I just want to get it done so that I can choose harder classes," she noted. As she wished, Ting ended up earning an A from ENG 107, and she was very satisfied. She decided to take ENG 108 in the following spring semester.

TO TAKE ENG 102 OR ENG 108: THAT IS THE QUESTION

Before making placement decision about his second-semester writing course, Jasim researched more on class options than he did when he made his placement decision in the first semester. When Spring 2011 course registration was approaching, Jasim was uncertain about which writing course (ENG 102 or ENG 108) he would be taking. During our second interview in November 2010, Jasim described in detail what went into his placement decision process. It was obvious that he paid more attention to the available placement options than he had in the first semester. Jasim gathered information about placement from various sources and managed to talk to and ask other students in order to know about their views on writing courses offered in the writing program. First, Jasim asked his American friends who were taking ENG 102 and ENG 105 and discussed differences between ENG 102 and ENG 108 with them:

> I was thinking of taking ENG 102. I talked to some people both outside and inside the university. I told them my point of view that I wanted to be in ENG 102 because I wanted to study with native speakers instead of with foreign students. I thought it is gonna help me more. Because I am in America, it makes sense to be involved with native speakers. (Jasim, Interview II)

After a conversation with his American friends, Jasim discussed English course placement with some of his international student friends. "So I was about this close to apply for ENG 102. I kept thinking about it. Then I talked to some of my international student friends. They said that the university made ENG 108 for foreign students. That means it is good for me, you know." Based on his conversations with his friends, Jasim had kept thinking about which section (mainstream or multilingual) of a second-semester writing course he should enroll in. When he met with his academic advisor, Jasim asked what she thought about his interest in taking ENG 102. His academic advisor said, according to Jasim, "You are an international student, it will be better if you want to improve your skills, and it would be better to be with native speakers." Based on what he was advised, Jasim came to his conclusion. "Okay, I am gonna take ENG 102 because she motivated me." It was certain that Jasim decided that he would be taking ENG 102 after meeting with his academic advisor. However, in the end, he decided to register for ENG 108:

> ENG 102 is gonna be more challenging and much harder because the instructor might think that all the students are native speakers and he won't explain stuff. ENG 108 is gonna be easier since I am an international student. ENG 108 is made specifically for international students so I think the instructor will be easy with us and explain more about the projects and things like that. So that is it. I just chose ENG 108 for that. I think it is appropriate for international students. (Jasim, Interview II)

Jasim's other rationales for taking ENG 108 included the following: "I would prefer to be in a writing class with non-native English speakers because I am gonna discuss with other students more effectively and I feel more comfortable about it than with native speakers." As expressed by multilingual students in Costino and Hyon's (2007) study, multilingual composition was where they could study and work with students who were *like* them.

I was also interested in how Jasim felt about taking a writing course with non-native English speaking students. He thought, "I am not gonna improve my English skills more than I am gonna do in English native speaker class." This was mainly because "we are from the same background. English is not our native language. When we fix our papers, there might be some kind of controversies because I think this might be correct grammar, those peers might think no, this is correct, something like that. And I ended up going to the Writing Center." Even though he thought there were some disadvantages of taking a writing course with non-native English speakers, Jasim still preferred multilingual composition because he did not have to be too cautious when it comes to speaking. Jasim explained that when he had a conversation with native English speakers, he always had to think before he spoke. He had to specifically pay attention to the use of subjects, verbs, and nouns. This was similar to what Afia felt about her speaking skills (see chapter 3).

When asked about his overall impression of ENG 108, Jasim replied: "The class is pretty good. We did a lot of research before writing." Jasim said he liked ENG 108 better than ENG 107 because it was more advanced and focused. "I guess this is my level, ENG 108 with international students. This is the right place. I feel more comfortable with non-native speakers." Jasim enjoyed working in groups, discussing and analyzing assigned readings. He also liked other in-class activities like peer reviews and editing workshops. "We have more interaction. I like it because if we work like in teams, we can have more skills. We learn from other people and learn our mistakes. I can know where my weaknesses are."

As the end of Spring 2011 was approaching, Jasim was close to finishing his first-year composition requirement, he revealed: "I feel released. I just wanna finish it. But I also feel that I need more English, because in English classes I learn how to take notes and how to write papers." Jasim seemed to be satisfied with his decisions to take the multilingual composition courses. "I really feel good because I think I improve way better in my writing. Before coming to ASU, I used to write only 300–400 words. Now I can write like 2,000 and more. That is an achievement, and I feel happy about it. I feel more confident in my writing," said Jasim.

I discussed in chapter 2 that Jasim did not receive sufficient placement information back in August 2010 when he arrived to the university. He did not know that he had options to choose writing courses as well as the differences among those course options, particularly ENG 101 versus ENG 107 and ENG 107 versus ENG 102. He did not know that international students could take ENG 101 and ENG 102. Based on his placement experiences, Jasim noted that the writing program and academic advisors should provide incoming students with information about different English classes. Here he emphasized: "Give them all information. Make them aware that there are other English classes besides WAC 107, ENG 107, and ENG 108 that they can take." Once students have all the necessary information, Jasim believed "they can decide. They may not choose ENG 101, but at least they know what options are for them."

Jasim also noted that it would be helpful for students if their writing instructors could inform them during the first week of classes that there were different options of first-year writing courses for students to choose from. Jasim described advantages of involving writing instructors in the placement of multilingual students into first-year composition courses. His comments implied that writing instructors knew who their students were. "Most teachers are native English speakers, and they work with both international and native English speaking students. They should know where each student is and his or her performance or whether international students are okay to be with native English speaking peers." Jasim's comment raised two important points. First, like I emphasize throughout the book, we should keep students informed about placement and its related issues. Second, writing instructors should be a part of first-year composition placement (see chapter 7).

Jasim also mentioned that there should be some kind of placement website and/or link for new students, or placement email announcements sent to them so they could learn more about first-year composition and course placement by themselves. When students meet with their academic advisors, they can ask them if they have additional questions and/or want some clarifications or additional explanations. Jasim's ideas are practical, and they are something that writing programs at any institutions can implement. In the context of the current writing program, the website and such information that Jasim mentioned was already available for students. However, it seemed that students did know about this source of placement information. Jasim's comments could allow the writing program to know what needed to be improved, and that the writing program should be able to make some changes immediately by making the website featuring first-year composition more readily accessible to students. It would also be helpful if the writing program and/or academic advisors could disseminate the website or link to students.

Jasim also noted that staff from the writing program should make a presentation on first-year composition and placement options at new student orientation. He also suggested that it would be helpful to incoming students if the writing program could share some placement experiences of previous students such as what courses they chose and why. Finally, as someone who had been through the process of first-year composition placement, Jasim encouraged incoming students to choose a writing course by themselves. His suggestions read like this: "If they feel like they are ready to take a class with native speakers, they can take ENG 101 and ENG 102. If they feel like they are not really ready, they should take ENG 107 and ENG 108. This option can benefit them because they are going to be around by international students."

WHEN AN EMERGING CONDITION FOR
AGENCY CAME INTO PLAY

Planning and questioning as the acts of agency were mani-
fested when emerging conditions for agency came into play.
To be more specific, the focal students' second-semester placement decisions were influenced by some other conditions
and/or factors. The case of Chan, for example, illustrated this
situation very well. It was not only sufficient placement information from various sources of placement that impacted the
way she decided to take a writing course. In her case, emerging conditions and/or factors like changing a major of study
affected her agency in placement decisions. While Chan was
certain about taking ENG 108 after completing ENG 107, she
also knew that she did not have to take a second-semester writing class in a consecutive semester. When Chan and I met for
our second interview in late November 2010, she had already
decided on her second-semester writing course. Chan told me
that she had planned on postponing ENG 108 to her third or
fourth semester; this was mainly because she had planned on
changing her major from business communication to accounting or finance. Changing a major required a good GPA and
some prerequisite courses, which she had to complete within
her second year of study. She wanted to delay ENG 108 so that
she could focus more on those courses. Even though she was
not sure whether she would be taking ENG 108 in Spring 2011,
she decided to register for the class. However, she seemed
uncertain about her decision:

> I am not sure about ENG 108. I still consider. Maybe I will drop
> it or I will choose another class because I can take ENG 108 in
> the summer session or in the following fall semester. Maybe in
> the community college because it is cheaper. And ENG 108 is
> not related to business. It is just English for foreign students,
> and everybody will take it. If I take it at a community college, I
> think it is okay. I may drop ENG 108 at the beginning of the next
> semester [Spring 2011]. I am still thinking. (Chan, Interview II)

In the end, however, Chan decided to stick with ENG 108.
Her rationale was well taken: "Actually, I was trying to take

ENG 108 during the summer at a community college. But my friend told me that the tuition fees between 12 and 18 credits are the same. So why did I have to pay more to go to a community college?" When I asked whether she was satisfied with her decision to take ENG 108 in Spring 2011, Chan replied with disappointment:

> No. No. No. I did something wrong. I should have not chosen ENG 108 for this semester. I don't know how to keep my work going on. I find it difficult. Something blocks my mind, and I just sit and keep thinking about the topic but fail to write. I don't know how to present ideas. This makes me delay my other work. (Chan, Interview IV)

Chan went on to describe her feelings about the class: "I cannot handle it. It is not perfect. Writing takes you a lot of time. Actually, I wanted to spend my most time or focus my attention on some courses required for my major." Chan said every time when she worked on ENG 108 assignments, "I just completed my papers before the due date. The class is in the afternoon, and I do my papers just before the class." She realized that she should have taken ENG 108 in Fall 2011 or later. Chan even said that if she could start over the semester again, "I would take ENG 107 in the first semester, but I would not take ENG 108 in the following semester. I would take it during the summer or winter break. So it would be easier to handle it."

Even though she was not happy with her decision to take ENG 108 in Spring 2011, Chan said she felt more comfortable with her writing compared to when she was in China. She also felt that it was easier for her to express herself when she wrote. Based on her placement experiences, especially with the second-semester placement, Chan recommended that new students do not have to take first-year writing courses in a consecutive semester. "If they are not confident enough, they can take ENG 108 in their second or third year when they are ready." Her rationale for this suggestion was that "ENG 108 requires more critical thinking. They should be prepared for this class; otherwise this course will be like torture. But I don't suggest dropping the class."

WHEN PLACEMENT DECISIONS WERE NOT SATISFIED

Another emerging condition/factor that interfered student agency was also observed in the case of Ting. She had planned on transferring to another institution; this also meant earning a good grade in an English class and a good GPA was important. When Ting realized that she would not be able to earn an A from ENG 108, she decided to withdraw from the class. In this case, the student exercised her agency when she was not satisfied with her placement decision.

Ting was happy with her first-semester writing course, but her second-semester placement was totally opposite. I met Ting for our third interview in February 2011, and there was a sign of her unsatisfactory with ENG 108. "The class is harder than ENG 107. It requires more critical thinking. We have to analyze assigned readings, using guidelines the instructor gave us, and write responses. We also have to work on good sentence structure, coherence, and transition words. I don't know if I can get an A from ENG 108," Ting revealed. She really wanted to get an A from ENG 108 because she had planned on transferring to other institutions. "Having a good GPA is very important," Ting emphasized. Ting's first semester GPA was 3.79.

When I met Ting for our last interview in April 2011, Ting reported that she decided to withdraw from ENG 108; this was mainly because she knew that she would not be able to receive an A from the class. Her decision to withdraw from the class was triggered by the overload of homework and assignments she had to complete every week. It was worse when she learned that she screwed up the first writing assignment:

> My paper is not so good. I only got 105 out of 150 for the first assignment. After I revised it, I got 125. I calculated the score and the average and my grade. I think it is not so good for my overall GPA. I will end up getting a B. So, I decided to withdraw from the class after I know a grade of my first writing assignment. Besides, there is a lot of homework. I decided to focus on my other classes. I will choose ENG 108 for next semester [Fall 2011]. (Ting, Interview IV)

Ting said she was not the only student who withdrew from the class; some of her friends also did the same thing. She spoke for herself and her friends: "We all tried our best to write, but we still cannot get a good grade. I heard that it is her [the teacher] first time to teach international students. Maybe she uses the way she grades native English-speaking students to us. Then, I think it may not be right for me."

In retrospect, it was not easy for Ting to decide to withdraw from the class. She recalled: "I think about this for a long time. I am afraid that having a W will influence my whole grade. But some of my friends told me that it is not a big deal." I asked Ting what her academic advisor had to say about this decision. Ting said her academic advisor "was okay" with her decision and recommended that she retake it next semester. Ting said that she had no regret about her decision. On the other hand, she seemed happier for having more time to focus on assignments in other courses:

> I think I made a good choice. If I did not withdraw it, my other classes would not be as good as now because I did not have time for other classes. Working on the English class' homework takes a lot of time. Compared to ENG 108, my other classes are more important. They are all my required classes such as microeconomics and mathematics. I think I made a good decision. I did not feel regret. (Ting, Interview IV)

CHAPTER REFLECTION

Exploiting their first-semester placement experiences, together with sufficient placement information they managed to obtain, the three focal students were able to exercise agency in their second-semester placement decisions by:

- questioning the differences among second-semester placement options (ENG 102, ENG 108, ENG 105)
- questioning whether taking ENG 102 would be beneficial
- planning on postponing taking ENG 108 for following semesters

This chapter also explicated emerging conditions/factors—such as changing a major of study and transferring to other institutions—that interfered student agency, making the focal students question more about placement-related issues and plan for what to do with their second-semester writing course. Chan thought about postponing ENG 108 for following semesters. Ting decided to withdraw from ENG 108 when she learned that earning an A would not be possible.

As demonstrated in this chapter and the previous two chapters, what went into the focal multilingual students' placement decisions was complex—various conditions/factors made student agency in placement decisions possible. In some situations, there were particular conditions/factors that interfered student agency. What we have learned from the focal students featured in this book will allow us to understand our students better, and I hope we will take what they had to say into consideration when placement is concerned. Since placement affects them tremendously, listening to students' voices will allow us to develop, streamline, and improve placement practices that are more student-friendly and able to address their needs.

6

ACADEMIC ADVISING
AND THE PLACEMENT OF
MULTILINGUAL WRITERS

*I always tell students that "it is not just this is your score and
what you need to do." I also encourage students to understand the process why they need to be in a particular class
and what they need to do.*

—Jerry, Electrical Engineering Advisor

Academic advising plays an important role in student success
and learning. Academic advisors' tasks, as explained by Virginia
Gordon (1992), are "to provide students with relevant and current information about curriculum, courses, academic majors,
and degree requirements" (27). Specifically, as Eric White
(2000) points out, "the selection of courses is the most readily identifiable activity of academic advising" (187). As I delineated in chapter 2, academic advisors' recommendations about
first-year writing courses were the most influential source of
placement information. In other words, the focal multilingual
students primarily relied on their academic advisors when they
were in the process of choosing their first-year writing courses.
To generate a better understanding about English course placement advising, which has been rarely discussed in writing studies, this chapter closely examines academic advising and its
roles in students' first-year composition placement decisions.
In doing so, I first share perspectives of the participating academic advisors on the placement of multilingual writers, focusing on how they advise students on English course placement. I
also include the voices of the focal multilingual students in this
chapter to share their views and comments on English course

DOI: 10.7330/9781607325482.c006

placement advising. Then, I argue how students are advised about first-year English composition placement needs to be improved.

Before I proceed to my discussion of academic advisors' roles in first-year composition placement advising, I feel the need to describe the four academic advisors' awareness of the presence of multilingual students and how they identify this student population. I believe academic advisors' understanding of students' backgrounds is fundamental to how well student needs are served. In the body of academic advising scholarship, especially in major handbooks of academic advising (e.g., Gordon 1992; Gordon and Habley 2000), topics like advising multicultural students and culturally diverse students[1] and suggestions for advising practices are included and eloquently discussed. For example, an excerpt from Gordon's (1992) *Handbook of Academic Advising* suggests that practitioners and academic advisors be sensitive to culturally diverse students and should understand that "each student represents a unique cultural background, including language, customs, manners, values, and attitudes . . . Advisers who are sensitive to each student's particular situation can offer the type of help and personalization required to help them adjust successfully" (132).

My interviews with the four academic advisors in the next section illustrate how essential it is for academic advisors to understand where their students are coming from and what their needs are.

ACADEMIC ADVISORS' AWARENESS OF THE PRESENCE OF MULTILINGUAL STUDENTS

For the most part, the academic advisors recognized the presence of multilingual students who were their advisees. For them, however, multilingual students referred to international visa students, even though, in fact, the multilingual student population could include "a wide range of students who are actively developing proficiency in the English language" (Matsuda, Saenkhum, and Accardi 2013, 73), such as US residents or citizens who are non-native English speaking students. To illustrate, two academic advisors reported on an estimated number of international multilingual students whom they supervised. In electrical engineering, as mentioned by the electrical engineering advisor, about 20 percent of students were international multilingual students; they were from China, India, Syria, Saudi Arabia, Kuwait, and Turkey, for example. This was the same with economics, which many international multilingual students graduated from. The field of math and statistics was also popular among this group of student population; and the academic advisor of this major said about 10–15 percent of her student advisees were international multilingual students. The math and statistics and business administration advisors were more articulated in reporting on a specific number of multilingual students whom they worked with in Fall 2010. While the former said she had five international multilingual students, the latter mentioned he had only a few international multilingual students.

There were various characteristics that the academic advisors used in order to identify international multilingual students. Students' accents and TOEFL scores were the most frequently mentioned among the academic advisors. For example, Keith, the business administration advisor, said, "they have thick accents and they have TOEFL scores." The same academic advisor also mentioned how he identified international multilingual students as follows: "The first clue I will see if they have TOEFL scores, usually not SAT or ACT. The second clue is that their English speaking ability is kind of broken. It is a good indicator but not always one hundred percent."

Furthermore, the academic advisors relied on records from the university's International Students and Scholars Office (ISSO) that collected international students' language backgrounds, among others. For example, the math and statistics and economics advisors mentioned that they knew and learned about backgrounds of international students from this office.

In some cases, the academic advisors knew that their advisees were international students because students self-disclosed.

As the math and statistics advisor pointed out: "Many students disclose themselves as non-native English speakers and mention a home country where they are from." However, when the academic advisors were not sure about students' backgrounds, they directly asked students. The economics advisor said: "I will just ask. I do not make an assumption. I need to be very careful." Like the economics advisor, the business administration advisor said: "If I am not sure, I will ask."

When asked whether they recognized who resident multilingual writers were, the academic advisors said they considered the following features to identify this group of students: accents, standardized test scores (e.g., SAT or ACT), and students' self-disclosure. For example, the business administration advisor said, "they have an accent from a non English-speaking country and they have either SAT or ACT scores." Based on her experience, the math and statistics advisor revealed as follows: "Resident multilingual students always self-disclose. I could make an assumption, but I do not always know that from having a conversation with students."

In short, the academic advisors were aware of the presence of multilingual students. They seemed to know who the multilingual students were and relied on various characteristics to identify international multilingual students and resident multilingual students. It was apparent that the academic advisors were more comfortable when identifying the international multilingual students. They had information about students' language backgrounds from the institution's international office's records to confirm their assumption. This was different from identifying resident multilingual students. The academic advisor participants had to rely on students' self-disclosure or standardized test scores (e.g., SAT or ACT) because there was no record of resident multilingual students provided by the institution. As Linda Harklau (2000, 36) points out, identifying resident multilingual students is not an easy task; and this is the case mainly because US higher educational institutions do not collect information about these students' language backgrounds.

ROLES OF ACADEMIC ADVISORS IN ADVISING
STUDENTS ON FIRST-YEAR COMPOSITION PLACEMENT

Before and during the time of this research, the studied writing program did not have direct communication about first-year composition placement with academic advisors and other related academic offices. I learned from the participating academic advisors that they usually received information about English and math placement from general academic advising sessions taking place early in the spring semester prior to when new student orientation began.

According to the participating academic advisors, academic advisors played an important role in advising and guiding students in general. One of the main reasons for this was that some students would definitely take their advice and/or want to be told what courses they should take. As illustrated by Megan, the math and statistics advisor, "a lot of students always come to me and say, 'you tell me what I am supposed to take,' while some students would say 'I expect you to tell me and I will just do it.'" Megan's advising experience suggests that students see academic advisors as "an authority" who "tell them what courses to schedule" (Gordon 1992, 51). In a broader sense, students consider their academic advisors authorities "in providing institutional and academic information such as curricular requirements, courses, institutional policies, academic majors, scheduling procedures, graduation requirements, and other aspects of the curriculum" (Gordon 1992, 56). At the same time, academic advisors play other important roles, including "expert, advocate . . . rubber stamp, judge, teacher, and friend" (Kramer and Gardner 1983, quoted in Gordon 1992, 51).

For their role in advising students on English placement, the academic advisors indicated that all steps of advising were taken to ensure that multilingual students were in appropriate writing courses and to encourage them to feel good about their English placement. More important, the academic advisor participants helped multilingual students to understand why they needed to be in a particular course. As Gordon

(1992) suggests, academic advisors' "obvious advising task is to place students in courses that are appropriate for their level of familiarity with the subject" (61). To illustrate, I share three academic advisors' reflections on their English placement advising:

> Multilingual students do not know what English classes they need to take because they are new. Our roles are to guide them to take classes that are appropriate for their academic level. (Keith, business administration advisor)

> Incoming undergraduate students do not necessarily know what English classes they should take. We just make sure that they are in appropriate classes. (Elaine, economics advisor)

> It is important for us to ensure that students are moving forward. I have to ensure that students be [are] in the right course for them. I also make sure that students understand that a particular writing course is the right course for them to be in. They have to feel good about it. (Jerry, electrical engineering advisor)

In addition, academic advisors helped students to understand the placement process. Jerry, the electrical engineering advisor, explained as follows: "I always tell students that 'it is not just this is your score and what you need to do.' I also encourage students to understand the process why they need to be in a particular class and what they need to do."

HOW ACADEMIC ADVISORS ADVISE STUDENTS ON FIRST-YEAR COMPOSITION PLACEMENT

The academic advisors primarily relied on students' standardized test scores when advising students on what first-year composition courses they should take. This was in line with the writing program's placement policy that determined first-year composition placement based on students' standardized test scores. Elaine, the economics advisor, mentioned how she informed her multilingual student advisees about English placement: "We begin from their test scores. That is really what it is. We go by test scores." Likewise, the electrical engineering advisor said: "I recommend English course placement to my advisees using their test scores, and I successfully convince them about the writing course they should take."

Based on students' test scores, the academic advisors communicated first-year placement recommendations to multilingual students. Generally, the academic advisors recommended that international multilingual students take multilingual composition and resident multilingual students take mainstream composition. Jerry, the electrical engineering advisor, shared how he communicated English placement to international multilingual students: "When I have a conversation with students, if they are international students, they have to do the [ENG] 107 in the first semester. They may do the [ENG] 102 in the next semester if they are comfortable with that." He also emphasized, "We mutually determine that students should do the [ENG] 107 or the WAC 107 based on their test scores."

Keith, the business administration advisor, mentioned how he communicated placement to resident multilingual students. "I would first try to get to know if students graduated from a US high school and I recommend that they take ENG 101 depending on the SAT or ACT scores they have."

Since the studied writing program used standardized test scores as a placement method, I was interested in learning what the academic advisor participants thought about this institutional practice. Elaine, the economics advisor, who did not believe in test scores, responded as follows: "I am not a big one for standardized tests. I do not believe in standardized testing, to be honest. It does not really measure your real intelligence. It measures how well you take a test."

Unlike the economics advisor, the other three academic advisors were advocates of the use of standardized test scores; yet they realized that test scores were not everything. Specifically, the electrical engineering advisor commented: "Placement testing scores are pretty accurate; they tell people where they need to be." Similarly, the business administration advisor said: "Test scores are pretty accurate. It is a good guide to where students' level is." The math and statistics advisor believed "test scores are pretty accurate," and she provided her rationale as follows:

I have not had students who were placed in ENG 107 and said this is so easy and I should have done ENG 101. For students who are placed in WAC 107, I believe it is appropriate. They are glad that they did. And I think it also lowers their anxiety because they know everybody else in the class is learning English as well. Some of them even say I love my English class because I know other people do not speak very well or struggle with the language like I do. (Megan, math and statistics advisor)

With the advantages of standardized test scores; however, these three academic advisors realized that test scores did not always measure students' skills. Thus, when advising students about placement, they also looked at their students' level of English proficiency. The business administration advisor, for example, considered both students' English proficiency and test scores. In addition, he always asked his student advisees "how comfortable are you with English?" For placement, he believed, "students themselves get to decide but I may guide them one way [mainstream composition] or the other [multilingual composition] depending on their comfort level and what their test scores are." Yet, he commented that students seemed not to have the opportunity to make their own decisions when test scores were used to determine placement. "Sometimes, there is no [placement] decision if students' test scores are low. WAC 101 or WAC 107 is the only option. This is different if students have high scores; they can have the choice," the business administration advisor explained. The math and statistics advisor had similar thoughts, reasoning that "the use of test scores is very black and white and there is not a lot of room for movement. If students do not get placed to one course; they go to the lower level course. And there is really not a lot of flexibility with that."

Since the Accuplacer Test was also used to determine English course placement in the studied writing program, I was curious to know how the test was communicated to incoming multilingual students. From my interviews with the four academic advisors, I discovered that two academic advisors informed students about this placement test while one academic advisor preferred not to do so unless students asked. For example, the business administration advisor shared how he communicated the Accuplacer Test to his student advisees: "I recommend that students take the Accuplacer Test if they do not want to be placed in WAC 101 or WAC 107." Similarly, the electrical engineering advisor stated: "For a student who is placed in WAC 107, I tell him/her to take the Accuplacer Test to prove if they want to be in ENG 107."

While the electrical engineering and business administration advisors referred the Accuplacer Test to their students, the economics advisor said she never wished to introduce it to her students: "I have to admit that even as an advisor, I do not like bringing the Accuplacer Test up unless I have a student saying, 'why am I in WAC 107? I should be in a higher-level class.'" The economics advisor went on to explain her advising practice as follows:

> For students who are not happy with this placement [WAC 107], they have to voice it to me. Unless, students actually come to me and say something like I cannot believe I am in WAC 107. Then, I tell them to contact the University Testing and Scanning Services for the Accuplacer Test. If they do not question, I am not going to go out of my way to tell them about the Accuplacer Test. I have no reason to. If they are placed in a certain level, I am not going to go upfront and tell them to do something else. Why am I gonna talk about it with them? (Elaine, economics advisor)

Furthermore, Elaine pointed out that many international multilingual students were not aware of the Accuplacer Test because academic advisors did not usually inform them about this test. As a result, Elaine believed that international multilingual students "proceed with whatever TOEFL scores tell them to take."

From my interviews with the four academic advisors, I was able to draw one common feature of English course placement advising: the academic advisors did not spend much time discussing first-year composition placement with students. Instead, they focused their advising on students' required major courses. One of the main reasons, as explained by the math and statistics advisor, was "when students first come in for their first semester, we are getting them oriented [to] the university and degree requirements and how to interpret what is required. We must properly orient them to how to access and use these tools more than discussing specific course choices in some respect." This academic advisor then described why she did not spend a lot of time advising her students about first-year composition placement:

> Being math majors, English seems to be an afterthought to them. They do not really . . . I don't say "care." But, where they [are] place[d] in English does not matter to them as much as whether or not in calculus versus pre-calculus. Their focus is on what math, computer, physics, and chemistry classes they are going to take. For English . . . oh yeah I have to take it because the university requires but I do not really care where I [am] place[d]. English is their necessary evil. It rarely comes up. (Megan, math and statistics advisor)

What the math and statistics advisor explained contributed to the existing body of literature on delivering academic advising services at different educational levels (Kramer 2000, 98), which described that "freshmen need help in formulating educational and career goals since they often lack the knowledge and skills to do this" (Gordon 1992, 24). Particularly, they "need to talk with, ask questions of, and try ideas out on someone with whom they feel comfortable and whom they can trust" (Gordon 1992, 24).

In sum, the interviews with the four academic advisors on their roles in advising students about first-year composition placement suggested that international multilingual students were advised to take ENG 107 and ENG 108, mainly because they had TOEFL or IELTS scores. Resident multilingual students, on the other hand, were directed to register for ENG 101 and ENG 102, mainly because they had SAT or ACT scores. This leads to an enrollment pattern: international multilingual students take multilingual composition sections and resident multilingual students are enrolled in mainstream composition sections. I am not suggesting that this enrollment pattern is wrong; yet, the fact is that both groups of multilingual students are able to enroll in any options of first-year writing courses if their test scores meet the requirement of the option they want to take. This placement information, however, was not well communicated to both academic advisors and multilingual students.

MULTILINGUAL WRITERS' COMMENTS ON ENGLISH PLACEMENT ADVISING

In order to have a complete picture of academic advising on English course placement, I share what the focal multilingual students had to say about first-year English composition placement advising. One major concern for first-year composition placement advising that emerged throughout my interviews with the multilingual students was that the students were not well-informed about English placement. This was confirmed by the academic advisors, especially when the math and statistics advisor commented that academic advising sessions with first-year students were mostly devoted to discussions about students' required major courses. The cases of Chan, Ting, and Pascal illustrated this concern very well. Chan remembered what went on when she met with her academic advisor. "We mostly talked about courses required for my major. We did not talk a lot about English because I know I will have to take it," said Chan. Ting had similar experience, explaining that her academic advisor "gives me more advice on math classes and other required classes for my major." Like Chan and Ting, Pascal experienced the same kind of advising. He described that he received enough information about other courses, but "for English classes . . . not really. I do not know if this is the advisor or if it [is] the way they do it."

In addition, inaccurate and partial placement information was delivered to students. To illustrate, when Mei first met with her academic advisor, she asked whether she could take ENG 101 and ENG 102. According to Mei, the academic advisor told her that those classes were for native English-speaking students. This suggests that the student might not receive accurate placement information from her academic advisor. In fact, both native and non-native English-speaking students can take those two courses if they have a required minimum score of one of the following tests: SAT, ACT, TOEFL, IELTS, and the Accuplacer. Unlike Mei and Ting, Askar said he received complete information about placement and available placement options from his academic advisor. "She just told me that I had choices of ENG 101, ENG 107, and ENG 105. She explained differences between each class and I said I would take ENG 107 because it was easier." Jasim, on the contrary, did not receive necessary placement information from his two academic advisors. "We need to ask them actually. They do not give you or tell you all the options you have. Meeting with advisors is about the graduation process and they did not get into specific details about English classes," Jasim said. Based on this advising experience, Jasim noted that, as a new student, he needed to be informed about other available placement options, not just ENG 107 and ENG 108. Afia was another student who was not informed about other available placement options in the writing program. She tried to understand that maybe her academic advisor knew that "I am not good in English so that is why she advises me to go to ENG 107, and I am okay with that."

The multilingual students also had both negative and positive impressions of academic advising. Because his impression of academic advising was not pleasant, Pascal said he would not need advising in the following semester: "I will just with myself [I will do by myself] and if [. . .] I am off track, I will go to my advisor," this is because "they [advisors] do not give you a lot of information, you know. I feel like they are just doing a little bit of their job, doing the cover, the surface of their job." It seemed that Pascal preferred to work with an academic advisor who was well prepared to address his needs. He then elaborated what he wanted: "I expected the advisor to look at my file and look at my score and say something like . . . oh, you got that [test score], you should go there instead of saying you should take this because it is a requirement." He also wished his advisor could ask him the following questions: "What do you want to do, what is your level? Do you rather want to be with Americans or foreigners?" Moreover, Pascal expected that "academic advisors should try to know more about students what they really want." The case of Pascal illustrates students' expectations of academic advising in higher education, and this emphasizes how important advisors' roles and responsibilities are. As explained in Gordon's (1992) *Handbook of Academic Advising*, "Students expect advisers to provide reliable and current information about the academic program in which they are enrolled, to know how and where to refer them to proper campus resources to solve certain problems (e.g., financial or health concerns), to be an expert on the institution's procedures and policies, and to be an expert problem solver" (52).

Unlike Pascal, Joel appreciated the way in which his academic advisor tried to understand his situation. "She is a great person. She participates in my academic decisions. For first-year composition courses, she told me not to feel bad that I have to take English classes again. I do not feel bad. I already completed all the required courses for my major, except for some fundamental courses like math and biology," Joel explained.

While the international multilingual students seemed to need English placement advising from academic advisors, the two US citizen multilingual students (Marco and Ana) said they did not need first-year composition placement advising and that they preferred not to consult academic advisors about it. Both Marco and Ana chose not to meet with academic advisors one-on-one before deciding to register for their English courses. Instead, they registered for their first-semester English writing course at new student orientation and decided on the second-semester English writing course by themselves. Marco recalled his decisions not to take advice from his academic advisor: "In my case, it would not hurt if I asked my advisor, but I would have gone with the same decisions either way. I think in the future if I choose beyond my prerequisites, I think it would be good to ask my advisor." For Ana, she simply said that she did not need to meet with her academic advisor one-on-one because she knew that she would take ENG 101.

The focal multilingual students' comments on English placement advising confirm my previous argument established in the earlier chapters that the focal multilingual students were not necessarily well-informed about first-year composition placement, particularly the available options of writing courses. In addition, the multilingual students expected their academic advisors to pay close attention to what they wanted and their level of proficiency and to recommend a course based on that information, not just from test scores. What is more, academic advising sessions were mostly devoted to discussions about students' required courses for their majors. It seemed that first-year English placement was taken for granted—this was the perspective of both the focal multilingual students and academic advisors.

CHAPTER REFLECTION

This chapter unveils how first-year English composition placement advising is done, using perspectives on the placement of multilingual students in college composition courses from the participating academic advisors and views on first-year English composition advising from the focal multilingual students. As explained by both the academic advisors and focal multilingual students, when the multilingual students met with their academic advisors for course selection and registration, they mostly spent an advising session discussing students' required major courses. They did talk about English course placement but did not go into detail, unless the students asked for more information or clarification. Meanwhile, placement information distributed by academic advisors was partially complete, especially information about available placement options and the Accuplacer Test.

In response to how the focal multilingual students were advised about first-year composition placement, I suggest that English course placement advising be reevaluated and/or improved. This advising practice needs attention, mainly because students always go to and primarily rely on their academic advisors when English placement decisions are concerned. It is essential that students receive accurate and complete placement information from academic advisors at both one-on-one advising sessions and group advising sessions at new student orientation. I encourage writing programs to improve and/or increase placement communication with academic advisors. When academic advisors receive accurate, complete, and updated placement information from writing programs, they can distribute this essential information to multilingual students. Simultaneously, tapping into student networks as a source of placement is something that writing programs can develop. As shown in the interviews, some of the multilingual students relied on other students' past experiences in taking first-year composition courses when making their own place-ment decisions. Starting to inform students better will enable them to provide accurate and complete placement information to their fellow students.

NOTE

1. In academic advising scholarship, multicultural students and culturally diverse students include African American students, Hispanic students, Asian American students, Native American students, and international students (Gordon 1992, 118).

7

WRITING TEACHERS AND THE PLACEMENT OF MULTILINGUAL WRITERS

Information about placement should be included in TA orientations and other meetings held in the writing program.
—Anne, Graduate Teaching Assistant

Using my interviews with the five writing teacher participants, this chapter looks closely at why and how writing teachers should be a part of the placement of multilingual students into college composition courses. I first relate perspectives of the five writing teachers on the placement of multilingual writers, particularly focusing on their knowledge of first-year composition placement and the placement information they wanted to be informed from the studied writing program. Through these explications, my goal is to address the following question: what role should writing teachers play in the placement of multilingual writers? Drawing on such discussions, I argue for involving writing teachers in the placement of multilingual students into first-year composition courses and then consider ways in which writing programs can make such involvement happen.

WHAT WRITING TEACHERS SAY ABOUT CHARACTERISTICS OF MULTILINGUAL WRITERS

The five writing teacher participants included two full-time instructors, one adjunct instructor, and two graduate teaching assistants (GTA), and they were the instructors of some of the focal multilingual students. They all had experience working with multilingual students in different contexts and settings

DOI: 10.7330/9781607325482.c007

before teaching first-year composition in the current writing program (see chapter 1 for the writing teachers' detailed profiles). Before I proceed to my discussion of writing teachers' knowledge about first-year composition placement, I briefly delineate some of the characteristics the five writing teachers used to identifying multilingual students.

Grammatical issues and mechanical problems in student writing were the first characteristics that the participating writing teachers mentioned when asked how they knew who multilingual students were. Here are their views on multilingual student writing:

- There are more language errors. (Anne, GTA)
- They often have mechanical errors, comma splices, fragment, and spelling errors. (Sammy, full-time instructor)
- As far as their writing goes, characteristics include lack of articles or misuse of articles, prepositions, and punctuations. (Beverly, adjunct instructor)
- Certainly, there is probably the language that is the most problematic for non-native speakers. Even if they are very good and a capable writer, there is a few article problems. (Ethan, GTA)

The way the writing teacher participants identified characteristics of multilingual students was similar to how writing teachers in an institutional case study of writing teachers' perceptions of the presence and needs of second language writers by Matsuda, Saenkhum, and Accardi (2013). In their study, some writing teachers identified multilingual students by their written grammar and the use of vocabulary. In addition to language-related issues, the writing teachers commented on how their multilingual students worked in groups or participated class discussions. While one writing teacher appreciated what her multilingual students brought to the classroom, two writing teachers agreed that group work and/or class discussion was a challenge for multilingual students. Their comments are as follows:

Multilingual students do bring interesting topics because they tend to look at things that are happening all part of the world. (Anne, GTA)

> When I put them in groups, occasionally some of them did not stay on task. (Sammy, full-time instructor)

> If I am using any kinds of collaborative or cooperative learning activities where students working together in groups, the multilingual students will tend to be very quiet and not assert themselves in conversation. (Dan, full-time instructor)

WRITING TEACHERS' KNOWLEDGE ABOUT FIRST-YEAR COMPOSITION PLACEMENT

Before and during the time of this research, there was no formal communication about first-year composition placement between the writing program and writing teachers. Given this institutional practice, the focal writing teachers, however, managed to learn about first-year composition placement themselves. While three writing teachers came across issues related to placement when they encountered cases of placement from their students, one writing teacher reported that he knew enough about placement in the writing program. Another writing teacher understood that academic advisors had the responsibilities to advise students on placement.

WHERE WRITING TEACHERS LEARN ABOUT FIRST-YEAR COMPOSITION PLACEMENT

The three writing teachers discussed their experiences with placement through the placement cases they encountered. For example, Anne first learned about first-year composition placement when one of her students was trying to get out of her developmental writing class. Anne recalled:

> I had a student who did not want to take my WAC 101 because she did not want to waste her time. She wanted to be in a regular ENG 101. That is when I got more information about test scores and placement. I have known now with my experience, not because of someone told me. They are issues I encountered myself and made me aware of it. This is how has been done. This is what happens. (Anne, GTA)

Like Anne, Sammy learned about placement from a student whom she believed was misplaced in her ENG 107 class:

> I found out about placement from one of my students whom I thought was misplaced in my ENG 107 class. It was a year ago. I had a student in my ENG 107 class and he spoke quite well. After two weeks passed by, his writing was superior. I called him up to my office, asking "what are you doing in this class?" He said, "Well, I did not have a choice. I was told by the advisor that since I was an international student, I had to take ENG 107." I asked about his TOEFL, and he said he made a high score. He also had SAT. (Sammy, full-time instructor)

Sammy further explained that, at that point in time, it was too late for the student to switch from ENG 107 to ENG 101. Through this placement case, the instructor later found out from the writing program that the student could sign up for ENG 102 in the following semester if he wanted. Here the instructor emphasized: "That was really how I found out about placement." However, "I [still] know not a lot about first-year composition placement." Sammy was uncertain about who was involved in placement decisions, so she made the following comment: "I am still not sure how much of it has to do with advisors who do not really know what they are doing."

Beverly also learned more about placement when she had to advise one of her students to switch from ENG 108 to ENG 102, even though in the end the student decided to stay in her ENG 108 class. Beverly recalled the moment when she met with her student: "I thought her English was strong enough [to allow her to be in ENG 102]. But she said she preferred to be in my class and thought there might be something that she could benefit from. And I told her she was welcome to stay."

Unlike Anne, Sammy, and Beverly, Dan was seen comfortable with placement. He revealed as follows: "I know enough to where I feel a student has been for whatever reason. I am aware that the writing program places students into ENG 107 or ENG 101 or WAC 101 or WAC 107 based on SAT or ACT scores or TOEFL scores. I know where to go and see how to match those things up if needed."

Another writing teacher, Ethan, said he knew "somewhat" about first-year composition placement in the writing program but did not make any further comments. Instead, he brought academic advisors to the table, saying as follows: "I believe academic advisors play such an important role when it comes to placement." He said that the majority of his students ended up being in his multilingual sections of first-year composition by recommendations from their academic advisors. "It seems that, ultimately, a lot of advisors encourage students to be in ENG 107 sections or in sections that are for international students." Ethan, however, thought: "Ultimately, it is their choice whether they want to be in ENG 107 or ENG 101."

Writing Teachers' Awareness of First-Year
Composition Placement Options

Since there was no formal communication about placement between the writing program and writing teachers, I sought to find out whether the five writing teachers were aware of the available placement options. The three writing teachers (Dan, Ethan, and Beverly) said they were fully aware of all the options that were made available to students, and each of them was able to recite each option. In contrast, the two writing teachers (Anne and Sammy) seemed uncertain about the placement options. As Anne revealed, "I am not completely aware of placement options that were available in the writing program. However, I understand that ESL students can try out mainstream sections if they want to. But, I do not know if the students know this or not."

Since Anne was not sure about the available placement options, she believed it was the academic advisors' responsibilities to inform students about placement options. She said: "I suppose they do go and talk to their advisors." Like Anne, Sammy was also uncertain about placement options, because "placement options are complex." Thus, she always went to the writing program office when she had questions about placement.

The writing teachers understood that native English speaking students had more placement options than multilingual students. In the context of the current writing program, in addition to WAC 101, ENG 101, and ENG 102, ENG 105 (Advanced Composition) is available for native English speaking students. There was no ENG 105 equivalent for multilingual students. As expressed by Beverly, "the writing program has lots of options for American students. However, we have more limited options for international multilingual students." Based on her understanding, Beverly elaborated: "So, for the American students, we have WAC 101, and ENG 101, 102, and 105. For the international students, we have WAC 107, ENG 107 and ENG 108. And it still feels like a lot of different language skills are getting combined together in those classes. It might not be such an awful thing if there was an ENG 105 equivalent."

However, Beverly was not sure how the writing program decided placement for American students whether they belonged in WAC 101 or a regular first-year composition sequence (ENG 101 and ENG 102) or even advanced ENG 105 classes.

> I think there is some confusion about which students are supposed to belong in ENG 107 and ENG 108 classes versus in ENG 101 and ENG 102. The confusion ends up coming from because of the course labels. It [the course title] says for foreign students. Even though students who are residents, their English are not strong. From what I have heard most of them end up being told they have to take ENG 101 and ENG 102 because only foreign students are allowed in ENG 107 and ENG 108. (Beverly, adjunct instructor)

During the time this research was conducted, ENG 107 and ENG 108 course titles were *English for Foreign Students.* These labels were problematic and sometimes misleading, mainly because they could prevent resident multilingual students from taking those classes. As research has showed us, US citizens and/or residents who are multilingual students do not always identify themselves as *foreign, ESL,* or *international* students (e.g., Blanton 1999; Chiang and Schmida 1999; Ortmeier-Hooper 2008; Roberge 2009). This situation is likely to happen, as

Blanton (1999) explains, because when US resident L2 students "reach college, they may feel strongly that they shouldn't be placed differently from other U.S. high school graduates, and are offended when labeled *ESL*" (123; emphasis in original). The writing program was aware of problems related to labels, so they decided to propose new course titles and descriptions for WAC 107, ENG 107, and ENG 108.[1]

My interviews with the five writing teachers demonstrated that while the three writing teachers realized what placement options were made available to students, the other two writing teachers were not certain about those options. In addition, the interviews suggested a lack of placement communication between the writing program and writing teachers. As a result, the five writing teachers wished the writing program to inform them and fellow writing teachers about all issues related to first-year composition placement. In the next section, I discuss what placement information the writing teachers wanted the writing program to communicate to them.

WHAT WRITING TEACHERS WANTED TO BE INFORMED ABOUT PLACEMENT

The five writing teachers indicated what and how placement information should be communicated to them and fellow writing teachers. The list reads as follows:

1. Inform writing teachers about all issues related to placement
2. Inform writing teachers about how placement information is communicated to students
3. Make placement information available to all writing teachers

To begin, the writing teachers wanted to be informed about all basic placement information, including: what placement is, who decides placement, and how and why students end up being in their classes. As Ethan elaborated, "I want to know what is exactly and how these students end up in my classes. It would be nice to know. Who makes decisions? Why are they allowed to be in my class, even though they are not that good?" This GTA also believed that for writing instructors teaching mainstream composition, knowing placement procedures could help them understand if there were "foreign students in their classes." Ethan, however, went on to comment as follows: "It does not mean they are all misplaced. Maybe they do belong there." Anne, another GTA, also shared the same concern, pointing out that "it is important that we make it clear what the placement is and how students end up in our classes."

Second, the writing teachers wished to know what and how multilingual students were informed about first-year composition placement. Beverly raised this concern and expressed that "I want to know what kind of advice being provided to students when they go to register. That is why I make sure I am giving them the same advice."

Third, the writing teachers wanted to see the writing program make placement information available to every writing teacher, suggesting where placement information should be distributed and discussed. Their suggestions were as follows:

> All writing teachers should be informed about first-year composition placement during fall semester convocations. This could be a part of a general meeting in August. The writing program could give a little handout about placement. (Sammy, full-time instructor)

> Information about placement should be included in TA orientation and other meetings held in the writing program. (Anne, GTA)

What the writing teachers needed to be informed about placement was reasonable. Obtaining accurate and complete placement information would definitely help writing teachers understand the dynamics of placement and other related issues. In addition, it could allow writing teachers to know their role and how they should be involved in students' placement decisions. In other words, when multilingual students need help with placement into first-year composition courses, writing teachers will be able to guide and/or advise students on placement procedures, placement options, and other related issues.[2]

INVOLVING WRITING TEACHERS IN THE PLACEMENT
OF MULTILINGUAL STUDENTS: A DISCUSSION

Drawing on the interviews with the five writing teachers, I argue that writing teachers should be involved in the placement of multilingual students into first-year writing courses. A follow-up question for my own argument is: how should they be involved? In response to the question, I began by closely examining previous work on placement that both explicitly and inexplicitly considered roles of writing teachers in the placement of students into first-year writing courses. Using what I learned from the interviews with the focal writing teachers, I then propose ways in which writing programs can involve writing teachers in different stages of the placement of multilingual students in college composition programs.

Let's consider the different placement methods that are currently available. Each involves writing teachers in different ways and processes. When written placement tests and portfolios are used, writing teachers' major role is to assess student essays; and based on students' writing ability and proficiency, a course placement recommendation is made. For post-placement, writing teachers may or may not want to reassess student writing by a means of diagnostic essays. A new course placement may be made in consultation with their WPA; this is done on a case-by-case basis.

The role of writing teachers as essay evaluators was documented in a placement process called the Writer's Profile (Lewiecki-Wilson, Sommers, and Tassoni 2000) in which students are asked to select multiple types of writing, including "lists, process notes, drafts, and revision" (170). In this placement method used at Miami University, Middletown campus, two writing teachers read students' writing profiles, "engaging in interpretation, discussion, and negotiation until they reach agreement on referral to the most appropriate writing course" (179). Lewiecki-Wilson, Sommers, and Tassoni (2000) developed the Writer's Profile in order to "help students and their advisors make more informed choices about course placement" (166) by incorporating input from writing teachers. The

Writer's Profile has also been used on this campus to replace the institution's use of standardized tests for placement. Lewiecki-Wilson, Sommers, and Tassoni (2000) made an excellent point that "the best placement decisions would be reached both through student self-reflection *and* assessment from those who know the curriculum" (168; emphasis in original), which are writing teachers.

In DSP used at Grand Valley State University, the role of writing teachers comes after students made their placement decisions. On the first day of class, writing teachers ask students to write short essays. They evaluate the essays (looking closely at student writing abilities) and let students know what they think. Based on what writing teachers say, students have an opportunity to switch from one course to the other if they wish. However, Royer and Gilles (1998) emphasized that the decisions to take which writing class should be made by students, not their writing teachers (58). In short, even though writing teachers have a say in the placement process, their role seems minimal.

In these placement methods, it is clear how writing teachers take part in the placement process. On the contrary, in the context of institutions with the use of standardized test scores, the role of writing teachers in the placement of students is unclear or even invisible. Those institutions place students into a certain writing course based on test scores they have. In the use of standardized scores, writing teachers' roles has nothing to do with placement. This comes to no surprise that some writing teachers may not be knowledgeable about placement. As I discussed earlier in this chapter, the writing teachers were uncertain about their knowledge and understanding of placement, so they requested the writing program to inform them and fellow writing teachers about placement and suggested how placement information be distributed to all writing teachers.

Building on this evidence, I propose that writing programs involve writing teachers in the placement of multilingual students into first-year composition courses. Specifically, I encourage that WPAs make writing teachers be a part of the placement process, assigning them the roles of placement informers and placement consultants. This can be done formally or informally depending on institutional contexts and concerns. As placement informers, writing teachers should be ready to inform students about placement and its related issues and to address any questions from students. As consultants, they should be able to: (1) explain to students how to choose a writing class that is appropriate for their ability and proficiency, and (2) describe how each placement option is different as well as advantages and disadvantages of each option.

Considering my proposal to involve writing teachers in placement, I maintain my previous argument that writing programs should communicate placement information to writing teachers so that they can relay such information to students. I believe writing teachers' roles as placement informers and consultants are relevant and essential; this is the case because they work closely with students and are the ones who can address their needs effectively. Yet, as I emphasize throughout the book, placement decisions should be left to students. What we (WPAs, writing teachers, and academic advisors) can do to make their placement decisions well- informed is to provide accurate and complete placement information and to be ready to address any questions students will have.

CHAPTER REFLECTION

Through the discussions of the five writing teachers' knowledge about placement and their suggestions for communicating and increasing placement information between the studied writing program and writing teachers, I propose ways in which WPAs can involve writing teachers in the placement of multilingual students into first-year composition courses. I argue that for writing teachers to be able to assume the roles of placement informers and consultants, they need to have a clear understanding of placement procedures, options, and other related issues. Thus, it is essential that writing programs communicate placement information to writing teachers and that placement no longer be as complex as it seems. There are different ways, as suggested by the five writing teachers, for WPAs to make placement communication formal and accessible to writing teachers in their respective programs. I would also like to emphasize that even though writing teachers are brought in to be involved in the placement of multilingual students, I maintain that students are the ones who should make their placement decisions.

NOTES

1.   See the Coda for changes made to the course titles and descriptions.
2.   In response to the writing teachers' requests for better placement communication, the writing program took action and made several changes to its placement communication policies. See the Coda for detailed discussions.

8

STUDENT AGENCY AND PLACEMENT DECISIONS
A Theoretical Discussion and Practical Recommendations

My quest for answers to my own questions inspired by Juan's placement case introduced in chapter 1 was the point of departure for the research reported in this book. The first-year composition placement experiences of Afia, Joel, Jonas, Pascal, Jasim, Chan, Ting, Mei, Marco, Ana, and Askar gave me and the readers a much greater and better understanding of how the multilingual students made their placement decisions, what factors influenced the way their placement decisions were made, and what went into the entire placement decision process.

In this chapter, I first recapitulate the major findings discussed in the previous chapters. I then explore, based on what was found, how student agency can inform the overall programmatic placement of multilingual students, and articulating a theory of agency I developed as well as scrutinizing how it can be applied in other situations. I conclude with some practical and research implications and recommendations for WPAs as they continue to improve the placement practices for multilingual writers in college composition programs.

MAJOR FINDINGS: RECAPITULATION

The major findings from my research showed that the focal multilingual writers relied on various sources of placement information when they decided to take mainstream or multilingual first-year composition courses. These sources of placement

DOI: 10.7330/9781607325482.c008

information included: academic advisors' recommendations, other students' past experiences in taking first-year composition, new student orientation, and other sources that provide placement-related information. Among these sources, the focal multilingual writers primarily relied on recommendations from academic advisors. Yet, information about placement from the academic advisors distributed to the multilingual students was partially complete. As showed in chapter 2 and chapter 6, the academic advisor participants did not provide accurate and complete information about placement options and the Accuplacer Test to the multilingual students. This affected the way the multilingual students decided on their first-year composition courses—the academic advisors recommended that international students take ENG 107 and ENG 108 because they had TOEFL or IELTS scores and that resident multilingual students take ENG 101 and ENG 102 because they graduated from a US high school and had SAT or ACT scores. This advising practice led to an enrollment pattern that has become common in the context of the studied writing program: international multilingual students tend to take multilingual composition while resident multilingual students tend to enroll in mainstream composition.

Nevertheless, at the same time, when the choice was left to students, the international multilingual students preferred to enroll in multilingual sections of first-year composition. Their preferences for being in multilingual sections resonate with preferences of ESL and multilingual students in previous studies (e.g., Braine 1996; Matsuda and Silva 1999; Costino and Hyon 2007). For example, ESL students (both international and resident students) in Braine's study preferred to enroll in ESL sections because they felt "comfortable or at ease" (97) when working with other non-native speaking peers who also had accents, among other motives. A reason behind this preference was that they did not have to be too cautious when speaking in classes because everyone else also had an accent. Like the ESL students in Braine's study, Afia was also concerned about her accent if she had to be in classes with native English speakers. As she once mentioned: "I like this class [ENG 107] because most of the students are not native English Americans. They are like me, so they speak like me, I do not feel shy when I speak to them." What was found from the case of Afia echoed with what seven multilingual students in the study by Costino and Hyon (2007) felt about multilingual composition sections, where they saw their classmates as someone who were "still-developing English language" (75) skills. Specifically, they felt that the classmates were international and multilingual *like* them.

For the resident multilingual students, they preferred to be in mainstream composition sections. In the context of this research, it can be explained that the two resident multilingual students (Ana and Marco) decided to take ENG 101 in the first semester because they did know about other available placement options and did not know they could take multilingual composition. They understood that ENG 101 was their only option. During new student orientation, both of them were not informed about multilingual composition options. What they were informed was that if they did not take ENG 101 from high school, they should enroll in ENG 101 in the first semester and ENG 102 in the second semester. It is worth noting that Ana's and Marco's decisions to take mainstream composition were different from other resident multilingual students (Chiang and Schmida 1999; Costino and Hyon 2007) who did not want to be enrolled in ESL or multilingual sections, mainly because they did not associate themselves with those labels, or they did not know what the labels meant to them. For the cases of Ana and Marco, they considered themselves to be native English speakers, even though they used their native language at home with parents. Both of them had a positive feeling about multilingual composition, especially Ana who expressed that bilingual and multilingual students should have more placement options.

Within the writing program itself, there was no formal communication about available placement options and placement procedures between the writing program and writing teachers. The findings on this part showed that the writing teacher participants wished the writing program to inform them and other fellow writing teachers about placement, such as what placement is, who gets to decide placement, and what and how students end up being in their classes. The writing teachers also requested for training and workshops focusing on issues in teaching multilingual writers so that they can be prepared to teach these students as the writing teachers realized the continuing growing number of multilingual students in their classrooms.

STUDENT AGENCY AND PLACEMENT DECISIONS

We have learned from the placement literature that directed self-placement (Royer and Gilles 1998) and the Writer's Profile (Lewiecki-Wilson, Sommers, and Tassoni 2000) are probably the placement methods that allow the most student agency, to differing degrees. Clearly, conditions for agency are built into the DSP system; these conditions are: (1) providing placement options to students, (2) explaining to students how each placement option is different as well as advantages and disadvantages of each option, (3) providing students with questions to assess their own writing skills and abilities, and (4) allowing students to choose which writing course that is most appropriate to them (Royer and Gilles 1998). Meanwhile, the Writer's Profile to some extent grants student agency. In the Writer's Profile system, students select various types of writing, such as lists, notes, drafts, revisions, and final drafts. Then, they self-reflect on their writing based on questions asked. Later, two writing teachers evaluate the profiles and recommend placement to students. Both DSP and the Writer's Profile are good placement systems; yet, it does not mean that agency does not exist in other placement methods, such as the use of standardized test scores.

Through the placement experiences of the focal multilingual writers delineated in this book, I argue that agency defined as the capacity to act or not to act contingent upon various conditions does exist in the context of writing programs like the current writing program that uses standardized test scores as a placement method. Student agency was found essential when the focal multilingual students made the decisions about placement into mainstream or multilingual composition courses. Each individual multilingual student demonstrated the case for students' voices in placement decisions, particularly in a placement method that conditions for agency are not built into the system. The use of standardized test scores—like other placement means, including placement essays and portfolios—does not seem to allow room for student agency. This can be explained as follows: when institutions use standardized test scores, placement essays, or portfolios, they use scores to determine placement for students and that, as it has been believed, students do not have to decide which writing course they want to take. Yet, even though conditions for agency are not built into this type of placement method, the multilingual students did exercise agency when they made decisions about placement. Conditions in the placement method of standardized test scores included various sources of placement information (chapter 2) and the freedom to choose writing courses. For student agency to be possible, it is essential that these conditions be made available to students; this is because students exploit various sources of placement information when they decide on what writing course is right for them. In addition to those conditions, other emerging conditions—changing a major of study and transferring to other institutions—were also observed, especially in the second-semester placement in which the focal students had a better understanding about placement. These emerging conditions, as discussed in chapter 5, interfered with student agency. I should note that the writing program, during the time of this research, offered a small number (eight to nine sections) of multilingual composition sections in each semester, the availability of seats in these sections might be a contributing factor that could also affect students' placement decisions.

Agency: A Theoretical Discussion

By using the focal multilingual students' placement experiences and drawing on what is found from the interviews with the academic advisors, writing teachers, and WPAs, I developed an alternative definition of agency and proposed it as follows:

> Agency is the capacity to act or not to act contingent upon various conditions.

My theory of agency contributes to existing theories of agency in two ways. First, it provides an alternative approach that considers conditions for making agency possible. Second, it involves acts, which is similar to agency theory defined by applied linguist van Lier (2009) and anthropologist Ahearn (2001) discussed in chapter 1. To elaborate, when conditions for agency are optimal, individuals have the capacity to negotiate, choose to accept or deny, self-assess, question, and plan. I call these "acts of agency." In the context of placement decisions, these acts, as discussed in chapters 3–5, are observed when the focal multilingual students exercised agency in their placement decisions.

When closely looking at conditions for agency, I categorize them into two types: necessary and emerging. The former includes conditions that are necessary, and I propose to call them *necessary conditions*, which are needed or required in order for student agency in placement decisions to be possible. This type of condition includes the freedom to choose a writing course and sufficient placement information from different sources: academic advisors' recommendations, other students' past experience in taking first-year composition courses, new student orientation, and other sources that provided placement-related information. Placement information from different sources refers to one that is made available to students and one that students manage to obtain. For conditions that are emerging and arbitrary, I propose to name them *emerging conditions*, which are unpredictable and changeable. They vary from case to case and can be anything contributing to student agency in placement decisions. The two emerging conditions found in the cases of Chan and Ting discussed in chapter 5 are great examples. In other placement situations, emerging conditions may be new ones or may not be found, depending on individual students' placement circumstances. Even though these two types of conditions for agency are specific to students' placement, these conditions could be referred to something else in other situations.

When necessary conditions for agency are optimal, students are able to exercise agency in their placement decisions, acting out the following: negotiating or choosing to deny or accept placement, self-assessing, and planning for and questioning placement. These are the main acts of agency. There are also additional acts of agency that may or may not be found, depending on emerging conditions as discussed in the cases of Chang and Ting in chapter 5. In other situations or circumstances, acts of agency may be different. Yet, those acts are contingent upon various conditions for agency. While I call such things acts of agency, other rhetoric scholars name them differently. Young (2008), based on her study of safe sex discourse, suggests questioning, negotiation, choice, and evaluation as fundamental properties of agency. These properties of agency, for others (see Callinicos 1988, 236; Flannery 1991, 702), are considered to be resources for agency.

Agency: Implications/Recommendations for WPAs

The placement experiences of the focal multilingual students highlighted in this book make the case for student agency with the use of standardized test scores as a placement method. I hope it helps us look at standardized test scores in a different perspective and a more constructive way. I believe what is learned from the focal multilingual writers' placement experiences can be useful to other writing programs. Next, I consider some programmatic and research implications drawn from the multilingual students' placement decisions and the theory of agency I developed.

Programmatic Implications/Recommendations

I argue in this book that student agency can inform the overall programmatic placement of multilingual writers into first-year composition courses. The placement cases of the focal multilingual writers demonstrate that when conditions for agency are appropriate, students will be able to exercise agency by negotiating placement, choosing to accept or deny placement, self-assessing when making placement decisions, and planning for and questioning placement. The key implication here is *how to maximize student agency*. In doing so, there needs to be improvement to conditions for agency, and I consider three practical ways in which writing programs can make placement procedures that both improve and foster conditions for agency.

1. Provide different placement options

First and foremost, writing programs should make different placement options available to multilingual students; this will be highly beneficial to them. For the placement of multilingual students, the most constructive way, as suggested by Silva (1994), is to provide as many placement options as possible (41). In the body of literature on placement for L2 student writers, current placement options of first-year composition include, but are not limited to, mainstream composition, basic writing, ESL/multilingual writing, and cross-cultural composition (see chapter 2; Silva 1994; Matsuda and Silva 1999; Ferris 2009; Jordan 2012; Miller-Cochran 2012). At the same time, other L2 writing specialists (e.g., Braine 1996; Matsuda and Silva 1999; Costino and Hyon 2007; Ruecker 2011; Matsuda, Saenkhum, and Accardi 2013) advocate providing different placement options to multilingual students. Braine, for example, specifically suggests that multilingual students should not be "compelled to enroll in ESL or mainstream classes" (103). Each placement option has its own advantages and disadvantages, and WPAs must disseminate this essential information about placement options to multilingual students. Like Silva (1994), I feel most comfortable with ESL/multilingual and cross-cultural options for multilingual students; this is mainly because their "curricula and instruction are, by design, sensitive to L2 writers' needs" (41). Instructors teaching those options are trained to work with multilingual students and to address their linguistic and language needs.

Previous and current research, including this institutional study, has also shown that multilingual students continue to find the existence of separate sections of first-year composition useful (Braine 1996; Costino and Hyon 2007). Yet, as I make this recommendation, I am aware that many US higher educational institutions do not provide separate sections of first-year writing for multilingual students. However, given how linguistically diverse US higher education has become, it is important for each institution to develop those separate sections for students.

2. Communicate placement information and make it readily available

Complete and accurate placement information is essential for multilingual students' placement decisions. I encourage writing programs to find communication channels that work effectively and make placement information readily available to placement stakeholders, including multilingual students, academic advisors, and writing teachers. Such placement information should include placement options, how placement is determined, and placement procedures, among others. I offer various ways to communicate placement information to each placement stakeholder.

2.1. Multilingual Students

- Provide placement information on a website and periodically update it.
- Disseminate placement information during new student orientation; this can be in the form of representatives from writing programs briefly presenting information about placement during new student orientation sessions.
- Develop documents, such as handouts or brochures, that contain placement information and distribute to students at new student orientation. These documents should be easy to read and understand as well as easily accessed.

There are two pieces of evidence that made me believe why distributing placement information to multilingual students during new student orientation is practical. First, my interviews with Marco and Ana raised a concern that not all students necessarily received complete and accurate placement information during new student orientation (see chapter 2). Second, from my personal experience as a WPA for multilingual students, I witnessed the advantages of distributing placement information to incoming international multilingual students during orientation weeks. At my current institution where I have directed the ESL writing program since Fall 2013, in the past it was not clear how students were informed about placement. During my first year (Fall 2013–Spring 2014) as a WPA, I had received tons of emails from incoming students inquiring about placement, its procedures, and other related issues. I figured out that such a situation was basically because of a lack of placement communication between our program and incoming students. Concurrently, I learned from my own research conducted in the ASU writing program that increasing and improving placement communication could allow students to make well-informed placement decisions. Beginning in Fall 2014, I developed a placement handout that included essential placement information such as how placement is determined and what placement options are available, and I worked closely with the university's international students office, asking them to help distribute copies of the placement handout to students during orientation weeks. It turned out that our writing program office received fewer placement-related questions from students. This is mainly because the students were better informed.

In case some international multilingual students cannot attend new student orientation, writing programs can provide placement information to them in advance by mailing them information about placement and other admissions information so that they understand what English placement is and what options they have.

2.2. Academic Advisors

For academic advisors, providing them a handout or factsheet that contains all the related placement information that they need to know seems to be a practical idea. When academic advisors have a clear understanding of placement, I believe they will be able to provide accurate and complete placement information to multilingual students. As showed in this research, the focal multilingual students mostly relied on their academic advisors' recommendations for placement. Thus, it is essential that writing programs develop communication strategies that can convey placement information to academic advisors more effectively. At my current institution, I developed a placement handout and distributed copies of it to academic advisors through the university's academic advising council. Anecdotally, academic advisors have been more informed about placement and able to provide accurate placement information to their academic advisees.

2.3. Writing Teachers

Establishing formal communication about placement with writing teachers seems to be one of the best ways to go about. Placement communication can be included in different occasions and events, such as meetings, teacher training, and workshops; this will help writing teachers understand more about placement procedures in their writing programs. In case students need help with placement, writing teachers can provide useful information to students. Writing teachers should feel comfortable sharing placement information with students. It is also helpful for students if writing teachers talk to students about placement options and procedures for moving to a different section if they feel they have been misplaced.

3. Allow multilingual students to make their own placement decisions

When it comes to placement decisions, students should be the ones who get to decide which first-year writing option is right for them. Both L1 and L2 writing specialists (e.g., Braine, 1996; Royer and Gilles, 1998) advocate allowing students to make their own placement decisions. While Braine (1996) argues "the choice should be left to the students," (103) Royer and Gilles (1998) point out that it was crucial for students to "make a responsible choice about which course to take" (55). In order for multilingual students to make well-informed placement decisions, I maintain that placement information coming from writing programs, academic advisors, and writing teachers must be accurate, complete, and consistent. With different placement options made available and information about advantages and disadvantages of each option provided, multilingual students will be able to make well-informed placement decisions. Equally important, we also need to be available to address any questions students may have and give them consultations about placement when needed.

Research Implications/Recommendations

WPA scholarship suggests that placement should be locally decided (e.g., Harrington 2005). For placement to be the most efficient, it should serve the needs of students in local contexts. Solutions that work at one institution may not work well at other institutions because multilingual students are different "from individual to individual and from institution to institution" (Matsuda 1999, 717; Matsuda 2008). However, I hope and believe that my institutional case study research and its findings can be an example or model for other writing programs to study and/or assess their placement practices for multilingual writers who are continuously and regularly presenting in college composition programs. I advocate conducting institutional case studies to learn more about our programs, students, writing teachers, academic advisors, and other related stakeholders so that adjustments can be made based on local and institutional needs. I, therefore, outline some research ideas for conducting program self-studies on placement:

- Conduct an institutional survey of multilingual students to examine their perceptions of labels, such as international, ESL, L2, English language learner (ELL), and multilingual, among others. In doing so, WPAs will be able to have a better understanding of what multilingual students think about labels and how those labels affect their placement decisions. What is obtained from a survey would be useful in terms of course title and description modifications as well as instruction and curriculum design and development. For scholarship on labels, the following resources offer insightful discussions:

Blanton (1999), Chiang and Schmida (1999), Friedrich (2006) Shuck (2006), Costino and Hyon (2007), and Cox et al. (2010).

- Observe academic advising sessions. An observation can be done during one on one academic advising sessions in advisors' offices or group academic advising sessions at new student orientation. This type of research would help us have insights into what goes on during academic sessions, particularly what and how placement information is communicated to multilingual students. An observation of academic advising sessions can be followed by interviews with academic advisors and multilingual students.

- Conduct an interview or focus group with different placement stakeholders, including writing teachers, academic advisors, and multilingual students in order to elicit their perspectives on placement and how it can be improved, among others.

POSTSCRIPT

This book all began from a very simple yet critical question: how do multilingual writers like Juan make decisions about placement into a mainstream or multilingual composition course? The question drove me to closely follow the 11 multilingual writers—Afia, Joel, Jonas, Pascal, Jasim, Chan, Ting, Mei, Marco, Ana, and Askar—who shared with us their thorough and candid first-year English composition placement experiences. The detailed stories of their entire placement decision process have made me consider the role of student agency in placement decisions and how student agency can inform the overall programmatic placement of multilingual students into college composition courses. In all, these multilingual writers' placement experiences are excellent resources for program assessment and improvement. Thank you for sharing your insightful stories. We will continue to listen to our students because we want to ensure that their needs are served.

CODA

I conducted this institutional case study research between Fall 2010 and Spring 2011 in the writing program at ASU. In the following academic year in which I wrote up my research's findings and implications and recommendations, I had periodically shared them with its two WPAs. While I was finishing up writing this book, I carried out follow-up interviews with the WPAs in early 2015 to find out what action the writing program has taken in order to improve the placement practices for multilingual students. In closing this book, I detail some changes that the writing program has made to its placement policies that are pertinent to multilingual students. Most of the changes, which are informed by the findings of this research, are particularly focused on improving and/or increasing first-year composition placement communication with multilingual students, academic advisors, and writing teachers. Each change to the placement practices has been gradually implemented, and the writing program has been doing this since Spring 2012.

CHANGES FOCUSING ON IMPROVING AND/OR INCREASING PLACEMENT COMMUNICATION
Changes Pertinent to Multilingual Students
- The writing program's website (https://english.clas.asu .edu/admission/first-year-composition-courses/placement -information) has been periodically updated to reflect current information about placement.

    The writing program's website is one of the main sources of placement information where students can find out about placement practices by themselves. It is necessary that the website is regularly updated and the information

DOI: 10.7330/9781607325482.c009

featured is accurate. In the past, there was an inaccuracy of test score information, which could lead students to misunderstand the options they had. For example, resident multilingual students would not think to place themselves in WAC 107 or ENG 107 because these two options required TOEFL scores. Similarly, international multilingual students thought they were not allowed to take ENG 101 or ENG 102 and that they automatically enrolled in ENG 107 and ENG 108 because they did not have SAT or ACT scores. Currently, the website is up-to-date; information about placement, such as test scores and placement options, is correct.

- A placement brochure was developed, and its copies have been distributed to incoming multilingual students.

  Between Fall 2011 and Spring 2012, I served as the assistant director of Second Language Writing in the writing program. One of my responsibilities included assisting the director of Second Language Writing in improving the placement of multilingual students in the writing program. Informed by what was found from my research, I developed a placement brochure featuring important placement information that incoming multilingual students should know. Such information includes placement options for multilingual students, how first-year composition placement is determined, and advantages of the multilingual composition track. Copies of the placement brochures (see Figure 9.1: Placement Brochure) have been distributed to incoming multilingual students since Fall 2012.

Changes Pertinent to Academic Advisors

- Placement handouts were developed and have been distributed to academic advisors.

  As one of the major findings of this research showed, the multilingual students mainly relied on recommendations from their academic advisors when they made decisions on what first-year writing course they should take. Thus, it is necessary that placement

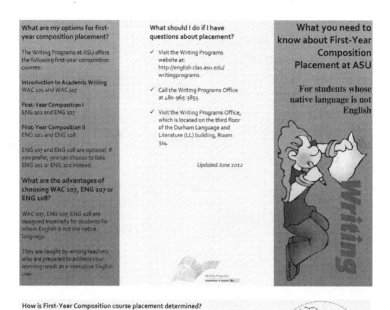

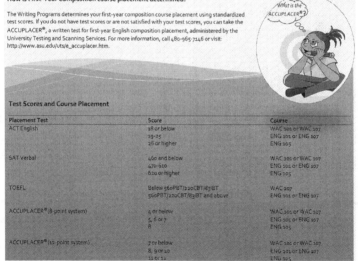

Figure 9.1. Placement Brochure. Permission granted by ASU Writing Programs. Art by Phillip Martin, Creative Commons Attribution-NonCommercial-NoDerivs 3.0 Unported License.

information obtained from academic advisors be accurate and complete. Based on what the findings of my research informed, I developed a placement handout that featured the placement information academic advisors should know. Some essential information includes a brief description of who multilingual students are, placement options for multilingual students, course descriptions, and how first-year composition placement is determined. Copies of the placement handouts (see Figure 9.2: Placement Handout) have been distributed to academic advisors since Fall 2013.

The writing program has also worked closely with the College of Liberal Arts and Sciences' Office of Student and Academic Programs in order to increase placement communication with academic advisors. In February 2013, the placement handout was featured in *Time Stamp Tribune*, the college's newsletter, which the target audience is academic advisors.

- Constant communication between the writing program and academic advisors has been in place.

Beginning in Fall 2013, the writing program assigned its new assistant director of Second Language Writing to work closely with academic advisors on the placement for multilingual students. Questions about placement from academic advisors go to the assistant director, who also regularly contacts academic advisors for updated placement information and other related issues. The writing program has also been emailing academic advisors, reminding them about the placement policies, emphasizing the fact that multilingual students have an option rather than having to take a certain section of composition courses based on their test scores. According to the director of Second Language Writing, a major challenge for working with academic advisors is that new academic advisors who are coming in are not always informed about historical practices. Thus, the writing program has to keep disseminating the placement handouts to academic advisors every semester. However, the writing program understands that academic advisors are trying very hard to do what is right. At the same time, academic advisors are using their network to spread the word about placement for the writing program; this is a positive development that is happening.

Changes Pertinent to Writing Teachers

- Formal placement communication between the writing program and writing teachers has been established.

  I discussed in chapter 7 what the five writing teachers suggested the writing program to do in order to increase placement communication with writing teachers. In response to the writing teachers' calls, the writing program has established ways in which placement information is communicated to its writing teachers. First, placement issues have formally been mentioned during the writing program's annual convocations, which take place every fall semester. Those issues include, but are not limited to, placement policies that are pertinent to multilingual students, placement procedures, placement options, and where to go if writing instructors have questions about placement of multilingual students. Second, the writing program has created breakout sessions at its annual convocations to discuss topics related to working with multilingual students, and placement issues are included. Writing teachers are encouraged to attend those sessions. In addition, when writing teachers have students who are misplaced, they are encouraged to report placement cases to the writing program, and that the writing program can move multilingual students to appropriate sections.

- A practicum course on teaching L2 writing has been required for writing instructors who teach multilingual composition courses for the first time.

  This L2 writing practicum course has been offered every fall semester and taught by the director of Second Language Writing. Required for writing teachers (particu-

First-Year Composition Placement Options for Multilingual Writers

Who are Multilingual Writers?

Multilingual writers are students for whom English is not the native language. They include international students (on F-1 or J-1 visa) as well as resident students (including permanent residents and U.S. citizens).

Placement Options for Multilingual Writers at ASU

	Mainstream	Multilingual
Introduction to Academic Writing	WAC 101	WAC 107
First-Year Composition I	ENG 101	ENG 107
First-Year Composition II	ENG 102	ENG 108
Advanced Composition	ENG 105	N/A

Multilingual sections are offered as **options** for multilingual students who need additional support for linguistic and cultural development. **They do not *have to* enroll in those courses.**

Course Descriptions

WAC 101: Combines classroom and supplemental instruction to teach academic genres of writing, including definition, summary, and analysis.

WAC 107: For students for whom English is not the native language. Combines classroom and supplemental instruction to teach academic genres of writing, including definition, summary, and analysis.

ENG 101: Discovers, organizes, and develops ideas in relation to the writer's purpose, subject, and audience. Emphasizes modes of written discourse and effective use of rhetorical principles.

ENG 107: For students for whom English is not the native language. Discovers, organizes, and develops ideas in relation to the writer's purpose, subject, and audience. Emphasizes modes of written discourse and effective use of rhetorical principles. Satisfies the graduation requirement of ENG 101.

ENG 102: Critical reading and writing; emphasizes strategies of academic discourse. Research writing required.

ENG 108: For students for whom English is not the native language. Critical reading and writing; emphasizes strategies of academic discourse. Research writing required. Satisfies graduation requirement of ENG 102.

Figure 9.2. Placement Handout. Permission granted by ASU Writing Programs. *Page 2 continued.*

Figure 9.2.—*continued*

How the Placement is Determined

The Writing Programs uses standardized test scores to place multilingual students into first-year composition courses. If students do not have test scores or are not satisfied with their test scores, they can choose to take the ACCUPLACER®, a written test for first-year English composition, administered by the University Testing and Scanning Services (http://www.asu.edu/uts/e_accuplacer.htm; 480-965-7146).

Test Scores and Course Placement

Placement Exam	Score	Course
ACT English	Below 19	WAC 101 or WAC 107
	19 or above	ENG 101 or ENG 107
	26 or above	ENG 105
SAT Verbal	Below 470	WAC 101 or WAC 107
	470 or above	ENG 101 or ENG 107
	620 or above	ENG 105
TOEFL	Below 560PBT/220CBT/83iBT	WAC 107
	560PBT/220CBT/83iBT or above	ENG 101 or ENG 107
IELTS	Below 6.5	WAC 107
	6.5 or above	ENG 101 or ENG 107
PTEA	Below 56	WAC 107
	56 or above	ENG 101 or ENG 107
ACCUPLACER® (8-point system)	Below 5	WAC 101 or WAC 107
	5 or above	ENG 101 or ENG 107
	8	ENG 105
ACCUPLACER® (12-point system)	Below 8	WAC 101 or WAC 107
	8 or above	ENG 101 or ENG 107
	11 or above	ENG 105

Writing Programs Contact Information

Room 314, Durham Language and Literature Building (LL)
http://english.clas.asu.edu/writingprograms
480-965-3853

The Writing Programs, Arizona State University
Updated December 2012

larly graduate teaching assistants, who teach multilingual composition for the first time), the course focuses on L2 writing pedagogies and strategies for working with multilingual students, among others. Placement issues and procedures for making adjustments after the placement takes place are also discussed in this course.

COURSE TITLE AND DESCRIPTION CHANGES

The findings of this research also confirm the problematic use of labels to identify multilingual students; this has led to another placement-related change that concerns the use of labels in course tiles and descriptions of first-year composition courses. As delineated in chapter 5, the labels, such as "ESL" and specifically "foreign" or "international," used in the course titles for WAC 107, ENG 107, and ENG 108 had caused the misplacement of multilingual writers, particularly resident multilingual students. The use of these labels has negative connotations, as explained by Costino and Hyon (2007), and "has been situated within discourse of marginalization and powerlessness" (77). In responding to such a problematic use of labels, the writing program in Spring 2012, led by its director of Second Language Writing, proposed new course titles and descriptions of WAC 107, ENG 107, and ENG 108 (see table 9.1: Course Title and Description Changes). The main goal was to ensure that multilingual students were placed in a more or less appropriate section.

The proposed course title for WAC 107 was Introduction to Academic Writing, as opposed to the previous one, which was Introduction to Academic Writing for International Students. The proposed course title for ENG 107 and ENG 108 was First-Year Composition, as opposed to the previous one, which was English for Foreign Students. The proposed titles were identical to mainstream sections (WAC 101, ENG 101, and ENG 102). For the course descriptions, two changes were made. First, the phrase "Foreign Students" was removed. Second, pre-requisite test scores, such as TOEFL, which included

Table 9.1. Course Title and Description Changes. Permission granted by ASU Writing Programs.

WAC 107	
Current title	Introduction to Academic Writing for International Students
Current description	For students from non-English-speaking countries. Combines classroom and supplemental instruction with intensive reading, writing, and discussion. Enroll requirements: Pre-requisites: TOEFL score of 0–559, ACT score of 0–18, SAT score of 0–460 or Accuplacer score of 0–4 (if test taken prior to May 12, 2009, then score 0–7)
Proposed title	Introduction to Academic Writing
Proposed description	For students for whom English is not the native language. Combines classroom and supplemental instruction to teach academic genres of writing, including definition, summary, and analysis. Enroll requirements: Pre-requisites: TOEFL score of below 560PBT/220CBT/83iBT; IELTS score of below 6.5; ACT English score of 0–18; SAT Verbal score of 0–460; or Accuplacer score of 0–4 (unless test taken prior to May 12, 2009, then score of 0–7)
ENG 107	
Current title	English for Foreign Students
Current description	For students from non-English-speaking countries who have studied English in their native countries, but who require practice in the idioms of English. Intensive reading, writing, and discussion. Satisfies the graduation requirement of ENG 101. Enroll requirements: Pre-requisites: TOEFL score of 560 or higher, ACT English score of 19 or higher, SAT Verbal score of 470 or higher, Accuplacer minimum score of 5 (exam taken prior to May 12, 2009 requires minimum score of 8) or WAC 107 with A, B, C or Y

continued

computer-based (CBT) and Internet-based (iBT) tests, were updated as well as SAT, ACT, and Accuplacer Test scores. In doing so, resident multilingual students would not be precluded from enrolling in ENG 107. In Fall 2012, the proposal to course title and description changes was approved, and the writing program implemented the proposed course titles and descriptions in the same semester.

Table 9.1—*continued*

ENG 107

Proposed title	First-Year Composition
Proposed description	For students for whom English is not the native language. Discovers, organizes, and develops ideas in relation to the writer's purpose, subject, and audience. Emphasizes modes of written discourse and effective use of rhetorical principles. Satisfies the graduation requirement of ENG 101. Enroll requirements: Pre-requisites: TOEFL score of 560PBT/220CBT/83iBT or higher; IELTS score of 6.5 or higher; ACT English score of 19 or higher; SAT Verbal score of 470 or higher; Accuplacer score of 5–7 (unless taken prior to May 12, 2009, then score of 8–10) or have completed WAC 101 or 107 with a grade of A, B or C)

ENG 108

Current title	English for Foreign Students
Current description	For foreign students; critical reading and writing; strategies of academic discourse. Research paper required. Satisfies graduation requirement of ENG 102. Enroll requirements: Pre-requisites: Must have completed ENG 101 or 107 with a grade of C or greater
Proposed title	First-Year Composition
Proposed description	For students for whom English is not the native language. Critical reading and writing; emphasizes strategies of academic discourse. Research writing required. Satisfies graduation requirement of ENG 102. Enroll requirements: Pre-requisites: Must have completed ENG 101 or 107 with a grade of C or greater

ENG 101

Current title	First-Year Composition
Current description	Discovers, organizes, and develops ideas in relation to the writer's purpose, subject, and audience. Emphasizes modes of written discourse and effective use of rhetorical principles. Foreign students, see ENG 107. Enroll requirements: Pre-requisites: ACT English score of 19 or higher; SAT Verbal score of 470 or higher; Accuplacer score of 5–7 (unless taken prior to May 12, 2009, then score of 8–10) or have completed WAC 101 with a grade of A, B, C or Y
Proposed description	Discovers, organizes, and develops ideas in relation to the writer's purpose, subject, and audience. Emphasizes modes of written discourse and effective use of rhetorical principles. Enroll requirements: Pre-requisites: TOEFL score of 600PBT/250CBT/100iBT or higher; IELTS score of 6.5 or higher; ACT English score of 19 or higher; SAT Verbal score of 470 or higher; Accuplacer score of 5–7 (unless taken prior to May 12, 2009, then score of 8–10); or have completed WAC 101 or 107 with a grade of A, B or C

APPENDIX A
Participant Selection

I. MULTILINGUAL STUDENTS

From 165 sections of ENG 101 that were made available in Fall 2010 in the ASU writing program on Tempe campus, I randomly selected 20 sections, using an Excel function called RANDBETWEEN. My goal was to get six multilingual students (three international and three US resident or citizen students who are non-native English speakers) from these mainstream sections. For the multilingual composition track, nine sections of ENG 107 were offered. I included all the multilingual sections in order to recruit other six multilingual students (three internationals and three US residents or citizens who are non-native English speakers). In the end, 29 sections of both mainstream and multilingual composition were a sample size for recruiting student participants.

At the beginning of Fall 2010 (early September), I sent an email invitation to students who enrolled in the selected 20 sections of ENG 101 and nine sections of ENG 107 to request their participation in four interviews. The writing program gave me access to the rosters of these selected 29 sections and students' email addresses. I individually emailed students under supervision of the director and the coordinator of the writing program. The goal was to get 12 multilingual student participants. I mentioned in the email invitation that students who participated in the four interviews would receive a $30 gift card when the study was complete, and their participation in the study would not affect their standing in their writing courses.

After a number of attempts of email correspondence, 12 multilingual students agreed to participate in the interviews. One student stopped coming after his first interview was completed.

DOI: 10.7330/9781607325482.c010

Another student also stopped coming after his second interview. However, I included this student in the group of student participants because he completed the first two interviews, which covered his placement decisions in both Fall 2010 and Spring 2011 semesters. It is also reasonable to use his interview data because the student did not indicate that he wished to withdraw from the study. In short, while this student participated in the first two interviews, the other 10 multilingual students participated in a series of four interviews conducted over the course of one academic year. In the end, there were 11 multilingual student participants in the study.

II. ACADEMIC ADVISORS, WRITING TEACHERS, AND WPAS

I selected academic advisors to be part of the research because they are academic staff members whom incoming students meet when they first enter the university, and they are the ones who advise students on course registration. It is important to know to what extent academic advisors are aware of the placement of multilingual writers into first-year writing courses. Because writing teachers work closely with multilingual students, obtaining their perspectives helps illustrate teachers' awareness of the placement practices of multilingual writers. Lastly, the writing program administrators address the current policies on placement of multilingual writers and other related issues. I recruited the three groups of participants by sending out an email invitation to request their participation in interviews.

APPENDIX B
Interview Guides

INTERVIEW GUIDE: FOCAL STUDENTS

Table B.1. Student Interview Focus

	Int. I	Int. II	Int. III	Int. IV
Time of Interview	Beginning of Fall 2010 (after Wed. of the second week of the semester)	Middle of Fall 2010 (after students register for Spring 2011)	Middle of Spring 2011	End of Spring 2011
Interview Focus	First-semester writing course placement decisions	Decisions about second-semester writing course (mainstream vs. multilingual	Reflections on taking first-year writing courses	Reflections on the whole placement decision process

Interview I

1. How did you choose to enroll in this writing class? (How did you end up in ENG 101/ENG 107?)

2. Did you know that there are different types of first-year composition courses for you to choose from?

3. Where did you get the information about first-year composition?

4. What did your academic advisor tell you about first-year composition?

5. How did your academic advisor advise you on first-year composition and placement options?

6. Did your academic advisor tell you directly which writing course you should take?

7. Tell me about your overall impression of your current writing class.

DOI: 10.7330/9781607325482.c011

8. What are the things that you like and do not like about taking this class?

9. What conversation do you have with your teacher about you being in his/her class?

10. Do you have any other thoughts you would like to share?

Interview II

1. Tell me about your second-semester writing class? What class will you be taking?

2. Why did you decide to enroll in ENG 102 or ENG 108 in Spring 2011?

3. What were other factors for you to switch the section or continue to stay in the same track of first-year composition?

4. How did your academic advisor advice you on the second semester of first-year composition?

5. How would you describe your experience in working with your classmates in your writing class?

6. What are the best parts of being in the class with native English speaking students?

7. What are the best parts of being in class with non-native English speaking students?

8. What are the disadvantages of taking the writing classes with native English speaking students?

9. What are the disadvantages of taking the writing classes with non-native English speaking students?

10. How would you describe your interaction with your teacher?

11. How would you describe your interaction with native English speaking classmates?

12. How would you describe your interaction with other students?

13. Do you have any other thoughts you would like to share?

Interview III

1. How is your class going?

2. Tell me about your experience in taking this current writing class (ENG 102 or ENG 108).

3. How does it compare to your previous writing class in the fall semester of 2010?

4. What are differences and similarities between taking first-year writing courses in the fall and spring semesters?

5. How do you feel about your performance in this writing class?

6. How would you describe your interaction with your teacher?

7. How would you describe your interaction with your classmates?

8. Do you have any other thoughts you would like to share?

Interview IV

1. I want you to think back to the first semester when you got here and you had to decide to choose/take a first-year writing class at ASU. Can you tell me what was going on? Where did you get some help?

2. Then, you had to register to a second semester writing class, was the process that you had to deal with easier? Can you tell me about it?

3. Are you satisfied with your decisions about choosing first-year writing courses at ASU? Please explain.

4. Tell me about your experience in the two writing classes you have taken at ASU?

5. If you could start over your first two semesters again, would you take the same writing courses? Why?

6. How much did your academic advisor help you decide about which first-year writing course you should take?

7. How much did your writing teacher affect your placement decisions?

8. What information has been useful for you when you decided to register for first-year writing courses at ASU?

9. What would you recommend new students about choosing a first-year writing course at ASU?

10. Do you have recommendations for the writing program to help you decide to take first-year writing courses at ASU?

11. What kind of information would be helpful for you when deciding to choose a first-year writing course at ASU?

12. Do you have any other thoughts you would like to share?

INTERVIEW GUIDE: ACADEMIC ADVISORS

The interview focused on the following topics:

Academic advisors' awareness of placement options offered in the writing program and other placement related issues

How they advised students on first-year composition placement

Their role in advising students on first-year composition placement

Their experience in working with multilingual students

Interview Questions

1. Tell me about your past experience in working with multilingual students.

2. Are any of your academic advisees a multilingual student?

3. How do you know that your academic advisees are multilingual students?

4. How often do you meet with your academic advisees?

5. Where do you receive information about first-year composition at ASU and the placement options?

6. Are you aware of different placement options that are available in the writing program?

7. How do you advise your academic advisees on which section of first-year composition they should take?

8. What are your criteria for directing or guiding your academic advisees to take which section of first-year composition?

9. Have your academic advisees ever complained about the first-year writing classes they have taken?

10. Have your academic advisees switched from a mainstream section (e.g., ENG 101, ENG 102) of first-year composition to a second language section (e.g., ENG 107; ENG 108) or vice versa?

11. How do you think your role as an academic advisor is important to students' placement decisions?

12. What are your recommendations for the writing program in terms of placement communication to academic advisors and students?

13. What information regarding the placement of multilingual students do you want to be informed?

14. Do you have any other thoughts you would like to share?

INTERVIEW GUIDE: WRITING TEACHERS

The interview focused on the following topics:

Teachers' knowledge about first-year composition placement

Their awareness of the presence and needs of multilingual students

Their experience in working with multilingual students

Their perceptions of the needs and support required of multilingual students

Interview Questions

1. How much do you know about first-year composition placement in the writing program at ASU?

2. Have you ever advised your students on what first-year writing course they should take?

3. Are you aware of placement options that are available in the writing program at ASU?

4. Tell me about your past experience in working with multilingual students.

5. Please describe your experience in working with multilingual students in your writing classrooms at ASU this semester.

6. What are the characteristics of multilingual students?

7. What are some similarities and differences between working with multilingual students and native English speaking students?

8. What does it feel like to teach native English speaking students and multilingual students in the same classes? What are difficulties you have had so far?

9. Compared to native English speaking students, do you approach multilingual students in your classes differently? If so, could you please explain how?

10. What are some of the benefits multilingual students can gain from enrolling in a writing class with native English speaking students?

11. What are some of the drawbacks multilingual students can encounter from enrolling in a writing class with native English speaking students?

12. What are some of the needs or support required for multilingual students?

13. What preparation, training, resources, if any, would have been helpful to work with multilingual students?

14. What are your recommendations for the writing program in terms of the placement of multilingual students?

15. What information regarding the placement of multilingual students do you want to be informed?

16. What information regarding the placement of multilingual students do writing teachers need to know?

17. Do you have any other thoughts you would like to share?

INTERVIEW GUIDE: WRITING PROGRAM ADMINISTRATORS

The first interview (Fall 2010) mainly focused on the writing program's policies on the placement of multilingual students into first-year composition courses and other placement related issues. The follow-up interview (Spring 2015) focused on changes to placement practices that the writing program has made after this research was completed.

Interview Questions (First Interview)

For the purpose of my study, *multilingual students* are defined as: (1) international students who hold student visas; and (2) resident students (i.e., non-international students) who graduated from a US high school and whose English is not their home language.

1. What are the writing program's general policies on first-year composition placement?

2. Does the writing program have specific policies on the placement of multilingual students? If so, what are those policies?

3. How does the writing program communicate placement information/options to academic advisors?

4. How does the writing program communicate placement information/options to writing teachers?

5. How does the writing program communicate placement information/options to incoming students?

6. How does the writing program work with other related academic units in communicating placement information/options to multilingual students?

7. What are changes, if any, that the writing program plans to make regarding placement of multilingual writers?

8. How can the placement policies and procedure be developed to meet the needs of multilingual writers?

9. Do you have any other thoughts you would like to share?

Interview Questions (Follow-up Interview)

1. Could you describe some changes to the policies on the placement of multilingual students in the writing program?

2. What are some changes that the writing program has made when communicating placement information/options to academic advisors?

3. What are some changes that the writing program has made when communicating placement information/options to writing teachers?

4. What are some changes that the writing program has made when communicating placement information/options to incoming multilingual students?

5. How does the writing program work with other related academic units (e.g., the office of international students) regarding first-year composition placement for multilingual students?

6. What are other changes, if any, that the writing program plans to make regarding the placement of multilingual students?

7. What are some of the issues and challenges when implementing the changes to the placement policies?

8. How can the placement policies and procedures be developed to meet the needs of multilingual students?

9. Based on the changes to the policies on the placement of multilingual students in your writing program, what are some recommendations or suggestions you could make for other writing programs?

10. Do you have any other thoughts you would like to share?

APPENDIX C
Main Coding Categories for Focal Student Interviews

My goal was to examine how the multilingual students exercised agency in their first-year composition placement decisions. In other words, how agency played out when the students made the decisions about placement into mainstream or multilingual composition courses. I began coding by carefully reading the student interview transcripts and made marginal notes in order to develop a general sense of the categories or themes that might be present. After an initial reading, I developed categories of how the students decided to take first-year composition courses in Fall 2010 and Spring 2011. The categories for the two semesters were as follows:

- Advisors' recommendations
- Other students' past experiences in taking first-year composition courses
- The fact that first-year composition is a requirement
- Students' preexisting knowledge/information about first-year composition (from various sources such as an online freshman orientation and a major map)
- Students' own decisions
- A combination of previous categories

Later, I created two coding tables: the first one for how the students decided to take the first-semester writing course (see table C.1: Coding Category for First-Semester Placement Decisions) and the second one for how the students decided to take the second-semester writing course (see table C.2: Coding Category for Second-Semester Placement Decisions). After the first round of coding, I had to modify these two coding tables.

DOI: 10.7330/9781607325482.c012

I replaced "friends' past experiences" with "other students' past experiences" because I found from the interview transcripts that the multilingual students also talked to other students who were not their friends. While "friends" was too narrow, "other students" was more inclusive.

RELIABILITY OF CODING

To test reliability of my coding schemes, I asked a second coder (who, at the time of this research, was a doctoral student in applied linguistics and had experience with qualitative data analysis) to separately code two student interview transcripts, which I randomly selected. At a coding training session, I gave him copies of the coding tables I developed as well as two copies of the randomly selected student interview transcripts. We began by reviewing the coding schemes to ensure that we had a common understanding of each coding category. I then explained to him the operationalized definition of agency and showed him examples of categories that I had already coded using the modified version of the coding schemes. A few days after the training session, I met with him to check the between-coder agreement. For the first student interview transcript, it turned out that we obtained 75 percent intercoder reliability for the first coding table, which was how the students decided to take the first-semester writing course. For the second coding table, which was how the students decided to take the second-semester writing course, we received 50 percent intercoder reliability. For the second student interview transcript, we obtained 67 percent intercoder reliability for the first coding table and 80 percent for the second coding table using the following formula:

$$\text{Reliability} = \frac{\text{number of agreements}}{\text{total number of agreements} + \text{disagreements}}$$

These between-coder agreement percentages were not unusual; as Matthew Miles and Michael Huberman point out that we do not usually get "better than 70% intercoder reliability" for the very first time of coding (Miles and Huberman 1994, 64). I then attempted at something closer to 80 percent code-recode reliability, as suggested by Miles and Huberman, for the coding tables that the agreement percentage was problematic.

I met with the same coder again to discuss the categories of how the students decided to take first-year writing courses, particularly focusing on one category that we coded differently, which was the students' preexisting knowledge/information about first-year composition. We looked at the student transcripts and tried to find examples that showed the category of the students' preexisting knowledge/information about first-year composition. We agreed that only sources such as an online freshman orientation and a major map were not inclusive. The coder suggested that the students' knowledge about test scores and their ability to find out about course descriptions of first-year composition courses should be considered evidence to suggest that the students have previous knowledge about placement. The coder raised a good point, which I did not pay attention to while I coded, and that I ignored these two examples. A week after a meeting with the same coder, I recoded the same transcripts myself and tested reliability of my coding schemes again using the same formula. It turned out that for the first interview transcript, the agreement percentages for the two coding tables were 100 percent and 83 percent. For the second interview transcript, the percentage for both coding tables was 100 percent. In the end, the problem of the first two coding tables was resolved.

From coding and analyzing the student interview transcripts, I realized that the multilingual students decided to take first-year writing courses using placement information that was distributed by various sources: advisors' recommendations, other students' past experiences, new student orientation, and other sources that provided placement-related information. When this placement information was made available, the multilingual students were able to make well-informed placement decisions. I considered the availability of placement information to be an important condition for agency; this condition makes student agency, which is the capacity to act or not to act, possible. The multilingual students would not be able to choose the writing course they wanted to take if the writing program did not give the freedom to them. The freedom to choose writing courses was another important condition for agency. In short, conditions that made agency possible included available placement information and the freedom, granted by the institution, to choose writing courses.

In the process of writing this study, I found out that some categories of how the students decide to take first-year composition courses did not accurately represent how they used those sources of information. So, I decided to drop three categories as the main categories, which included: the fact that first-year composition is required, students' preexisting knowledge/information about first-year composition, and students' own decisions. In addition, I inductively created two new categories, which were: new student orientation and other sources that provide placement-related information. I did not really eliminate those three categories. Instead, I assigned them to be part of the two new categories. The category "the fact that first-year composition is required" was part of the category "other sources that provide placement related information." The category "students' preexisting knowledge/information about first-year composition" was also part of the category "other sources that provide placement related information." For the category "students' own decisions," I eliminated it as the main category, but it could be part of any other main categories because when the students received information about placement from various sources, they made decisions based on the information they had.

REFLECTIONS ON HOW THEORY OF
AGENCY IS DEVELOPED

While developing my definition of agency, I discovered the following: when the conditions for agency were appropriate, the multilingual student participants were able to negotiate their placement, choose to accept or deny their original placement, question their placement, plan for placement, self-assess their proficiency level as they chose a writing course, and make decisions about a writing course they wanted to take. I call these abilities *"acts of agency."* Yet, this did not mean that I did not use a framework for coding and analyzing. In fact, I first coded the interview transcripts and looked for acts of agency using existing definitions of agency by scholars in the fields of anthropology (e.g., Ahearn 2001), rhetoric (e.g., Callinicos 1988; Flannery 1991; Hauser 2004; Young 2008), and applied linguistics (e.g., van Lier 2009). Primarily relying on the existing definitions of agency, I created two coding tables: the first one listed resources for agency (see table C.3: Coding Category for Agency Resources); the second one listed agency requirements (see table C.4: Coding Category for Agency Requirements). When I coded, I found that the categories in the two coding tables were very constraining, and I found them very problematic. I realized that I did not really want to look for agency resources and agency requirements. On the contrary, my analysis goal was to look for acts of agency. Later, I figured that these two coding tables did not work and so decided not to use them. I then started the coding over and ended up relying on emerging patterns and inductive analysis.

TABLES FOR CODING CATEGORIES

Table C.1. Coding Category for First-Semester Placement Decisions

How the students decided to take the first-semester composition course. Please put a plus sign to indicate evidence/examples for each category.

Name (pseudonym)	1*	2*	3*	4*	5*	6*
Ana						
Askar						
Afia						
Jasim						
Joel						

continued

Table C.1—*continued*

Name (pseudonym)	1*	2*	3*	4*	5*	6*
Marco						
Pascal						
Chan						
Ting						
Mei						
Jonas						

*1 = Advisors' recommendations; 2 = Other students' past experiences in taking FYC; 3 = The fact that FYC is the requirement; 4 = Students' preexisting knowledge/information about FYC (major map, DARS, online orientation); 5 = Students' own decisions; 6 = A combination of previous factors

Table C.2. Coding Category for Second-Semester Placement Decisions

How the students decided to take the second-semester composition course. Please put a plus sign to indicate evidence/examples for each category.

Name (pseudonym)	1*	2*	3*	4*	5*	6*
Ana						
Askar						
Afia						
Jasim						
Joel						
Marco						
Pascal						
Chan						
Ting						
Mei						
Jonas						

*1 = Advisors' recommendations; 2 = Other students' past experiences in taking FYC; 3 = The fact that FYC is the requirement; 4 = Students' preexisting knowledge/information about FYC (major map, DARS, online orientation); 5 = Students' own decisions; 6 = A combination of previous factors

Table C.3. Coding Category for Agency Resources

Resources of agency include choice, questioning, and negotiation.
Please put a plus sign to indicate evidence/examples of agency resources.

Name (pseudonym)	Choice	Questioning	Negotiation
Ana			
Askar			
Afia			
Jasim			
Joel			
Marco			
Pascal			
Chan			
Ting			
Mei			
Jonas			

Table C.4. Coding Category for Agency Requirements

Agency requires planning, self-evaluating, and decision-making.
Please put a plus sign to indicate evidence/examples of one's capacity to act,
including planning, self-evaluating, and decision-making.

Name (pseudonym)	Planning	Self-Evaluating	Decision-Making
Ana			
Askar			
Afia			
Jasim			
Joel			
Marco			
Pascal			
Chan			
Ting			
Mei			
Jonas			

REFERENCES

"2015 Open Doors Report on International Educational Exchange." 2015. *iie. org*, November 16. http://www.iie.org/Who-We-Are/News-and-Events/Press -Center/Press-Releases/2015/2015-11-16-Open-Doors-Data.

Ahearn, Laura. 2001. "Language and Agency." *Annual Review of Anthropology* 30 (1): 109–37. http://dx.doi.org/10.1146/annurev.anthro.30.1.109.

Anderson, Perry R. 1980. *Arguments within English Marxism.* New York: Verso.

Belanoff, Pat. 1991. "The Myths of Assessment." *Journal of Basic Writing* 10 (1): 54–66.

Blanton, Linda. 1999. "Classroom Instruction and Language Minority Students: On Teaching to 'Smarter' Readers and Writers." In *Generation 1.5 Meets College Composition: Issues in the Teaching of Writing to US-Educated Learners of ESL*, ed. Linda Harklau, Kay M. Losey, and Meryl Siegal, 119–42. Mahwah, NJ: Lawrence Erlbaum Associates.

Braine, George. 1996. "ESL Students in First-Year Writing Courses: ESL Versus Mainstream Classes." *Journal of Second Language Writing* 5 (2): 91–107. http:// dx.doi.org/10.1016/S1060-3743(96)90020-X.

Breland, Hunter. 1977. "Can Multiple-Choice Tests Measure Writing Skills?" *College Board Review* 103:11–5.

Callinicos, Alex. 1988. *Making History: Agency, Structure, and Change in Social Theory.* Ithaca: Cornell University Press.

Campbell, Karlyn. 2005. "Agency: Promiscuous and Protean." *Communication and Critical/Cultural Studies* 2 (1): 1–19. http://dx.doi.org/10.1080/14791420420 00332134.

CCCC Statement on Second Language Writing and Writers. 2009. http://www .ncte.org/cccc/resources/positions/secondlangwriting.

Chiang, Yuet-Sim, and Mary Schmida. 1999. "Language Identity and Language Ownership: Linguistic Conflicts of First-Year University Writing Students." In *Generation 1.5 Meets College Composition: Issues in the Teaching of Writing to US-Educated Learners of ESL*, ed. Linda Harklau, Kay M. Losey, and Meryl Siegal, 81–96. Mahwah, NJ: Lawrence Erlbaum Associates.

Costino, Kimberly, and Sunny Hyon. 2007. "'A Class for Students Like Me': Reconsidering Relationships Among Identity Labels, Residency Status, and Students' Preferences for Mainstream or Multilingual Composition." *Journal of Second Language Writing* 16 (2): 63–81. http://dx.doi.org/10.1016/j.jslw .2007.04.001.

Cox, Michelle, Jay Jordan, Christina Ortmeier-Hooper, and Gwen Gray Schwartz, eds. 2010. *Reinventing Identities in Second Language Writing.* Urbana: National Council of Teachers of English.

DOI: 10.7330/9781607325482.c013

Crusan, Deborah. 2002. "An Assessment of ESL Writing Placement Assessment." *Assessing Writing* 8 (1): 17–30. http://dx.doi.org/10.1016/S1075-2935(02)00 028-4.

Crusan, Deborah, and Carol Cornett. 2002. "The Cart before the Horse: Teaching Assessment Criteria before Writing." *The International Journal for Teachers of English Writing Skills* 9: 20–33.

Crusan, Deborah. 2006. "The Politics of Implementing Online Directed Self-Placement for Second Language Writers." In *The Politics of Second Language Writing: In Search of the Promised Land*, ed. Paul Kei Matsuda, Christina Ortmeier-Hooper, and Xiaoye You, 205–21. West Lafayette, IN: Parlor Press.

Elbow, Peter. 1997. "Writing Assessment in the Twenty-First Century: A Utopian View." In *Composition in the 21st Century: Crisis and Changes*, ed. Lynn Boom, Donald Daiker, and Edward White, 83–100. Carbondale: Southern Illinois University Press.

Ferretti, Eileen. 2001. "Just A Little Higher Education: Teaching Working-Class Women on the Vocational Track." In *The Politics of Writing in the Two-Year College*, ed. Barry Alford and Keith Kroll, 1–18. Portsmouth, NH: Heinemann.

Ferris, Dana. 2009. *Teaching College Writing to Diverse Student Populations.* Ann Arbor: University of Michigan Press. http://dx.doi.org/10.3998/mpub.263445.

Flannery, Kathryn. 1991. "Review: Composition and the Question of Agency." *College English* 53 (6): 701–13. http://dx.doi.org/10.2307/377895.

Friedrich, Patricia. 2006. "Assessing the Needs of Linguistically Diverse First-Year Students: Bringing Together and Telling Apart International ESL, Resident ESL and Monolingual Basic Writers." *WPA: Writing Program Administration* 30 (1/2): 15–35.

Glau, Greg R. 2007. "Stretch at 10: A Progress Report on Arizona State University's Stretch Program." *Journal of Basic Writing* 26 (2): 30–48.

Gordon, Barbara. 1987. "Another Look: Standardized Tests for Placement in College Composition Courses." *WPA: Writing Program Administration* 10 (3): 29–38.

Gordon, Virginia. 1992. *Handbook of Academic Advising.* Westport, CT: Greenwood Press.

Gordon, Virginia, and Wesley R. Habley, eds. 2000. *Academic Advising: A Comprehensive Handbook.* San Francisco: Jossey-Bass Inc., Publishers.

Greenberg, Karen, Harvey Wiener, and Richard A. Donovan. 1986. *Writing Assessment: Issues and Strategies.* New York: Longman.

Grego, Rhonda, and Nancy Thompson. 1995. "The Writing Studio Program: Reconfiguring Basic Writing/Freshman Writing." *WPA: Writing Program Administration* 19 (1/2): 66–79.

Grego, Rhonda, and Nancy Thompson. 1996. "Repositioning Remediation: Renegotiating Composition's Work in the Academy." *College Composition and Communication* 47 (1): 62–84. http://dx.doi.org/10.2307/358274.

Harklau, Linda. 2000. "From the 'Good Kids' to the 'Worst': Representations of English Language Learners Across Educational Settings." *TESOL Quarterly* 34 (1): 35–67. http://dx.doi.org/10.2307/3588096.

Harklau, Linda, Kay Losey, and Meryl Siegal, eds. 1999. *Generation 1.5 Meets College Composition: Issues in the Teaching of Writing to US-Educated Leaners of ESL.* Mahwah, NJ: Lawrence Erlbaum.

Harrington, Susanmarie. 2005. "Learning of Ride the Waves: Making Decisions about Placement Testing." *WPA: Writing Program Administration* 28 (3): 9–29.

Harter, Susan. 1999. *The Construction of the Self: A Developmental Perspective.* New York: The Guilford Press.

Haswell, Richard. 1998. "Searching for Kiyoko: Bettering Mandatory ESL Writing Placement." *Journal of Second Language Writing* 7 (2): 133–74. http://dx.doi.org/10.1016/S1060-3743(98)90011-X.

Hauser, Gerard. 2004. "Editor's Introduction." *Philosophy & Rhetoric* 37 (3): 181–7. http://dx.doi.org/10.1353/par.2004.0022.

Huot, Brian. 1990. "Reliability, Validity, and Holistic Scoring: What We Know and What We Need to Know." *College Composition and Communication* 41 (2): 201–13. http://dx.doi.org/10.2307/358160.

Huot, Brian. 1994. "A Survey of College and University Writing Placement Practices." *WPA: Writing Program Administration* 17 (3): 49–65.

Jordan, Jay. 2012. *Redesigning Composition for Multilingual Realities.* Urbana: NCTE.

King, Nancy. 2011. "Advising Delivery: Group Strategies." In *Academic Advising: A Comprehensive Handbook*, ed. Virginia Gordon, Wesley Habley, and Thomas Grites, 279–91. San Francisco: Jossey-Bass.

Koerber, Amy. 2006. "Rhetorical Agency, Resistance, and the Disciplinary Rhetorics of Breastfeeding." *Technical Communication Quarterly* 15 (1): 87–101. http://dx.doi.org/10.1207/s15427625tcq1501_7.

Kramer, Gary. 2000. "Advising Students at Different Educational Levels." In *Academic Advising: A Comprehensive Handbook*, ed. Virginia Gordon and Wesley R. Habley, 84–104. San Francisco: Jossey-Bass Inc.

Kramer, Howard, and Robert Gardner. 1983. *Advising by Faculty.* Washington, DC: National Education Association.

Kruger, Justin, and David Dunning. 1999. "Unskilled and Unaware of It: How Difficulties in Recognizing One's Own Competence Leads to Inflated Self-Assessments." *Journal of Personality and Social Psychology* 77 (6): 1121–34. http://dx.doi.org/10.1037/0022-3514.77.6.1121.

Leki, Ilona. 1991. "A New Approach to Advanced ESL Placement Testing." *WPA: Writing Program Administration* 14 (3): 53–68.

Leki, Ilona. 2007. *Undergraduates in a Second Language: Challenges and Complexities of Academic Literacy Development.* New York: Lawrence Erlbaum Associates.

Lewiecki-Wilson, Cynthia, Jeff Sommers, and John Paul Tassoni. 2000. "Rhetoric and the Writer's Profile: Problematizing Directed Self-Placement." *Assessing Writing* 7 (2): 165–83. http://dx.doi.org/10.1016/S1075-2935(00)00020-9.

Matsuda, Paul Kei. 1999. "Composition Studies and ESL Writing: A Disciplinary Division of Labor." *College Composition and Communication* 50 (4): 699–721.

Matsuda, Paul Kei. 2008. "Myth 8: International and U.S. Resident ESL Writers Cannot Be Taught in the Same Class." In *Writing Myths: Applying Second Language Research to Classroom Teaching*, ed. Joy Reid, 159–76. Ann Arbor: University of Michigan Press.

Matsuda, Paul Kei, and Tony Silva. 1999. "Cross-Cultural Composition: Mediated Integration of US and International Students." *Composition Studies* 27 (1): 15–30.

Matsuda, Paul Kei, Tanita Saenkhum, and Steven Accardi. 2013. "Writing Teachers' Perceptions of the Presence and Needs of Second Language Writers: An Institutional Case Study." *Journal of Second Language Writing* 22 (1): 68–86. http://dx.doi.org/10.1016/j.jslw.2012.10.001.

Matzen, Richard N., and Jeff E. Hoyt. 2004. "Basic Writing Placement with Holistically Scored Essays: Research Evidence." *Journal of Developmental Education* 28 (1): 2–12.

Miles, Matthew B., and Michael Huberman. 1994. *Qualitative Data Analysis: An Expanded Sourcebook.* Thousand Oaks, CA: Sage Publications.

Miller-Cochran, Susan. 2012. "Beyond 'ESL Writing': Teaching Cross-Cultural Composition at a Community College." *Teaching English in the Two-Year College* 40 (1): 20–30.

Ortmeier-Hooper, Christina. 2008. "'English May Be My Second Language, But I'm Not 'ESL.'" *College Composition and Communication* 59 (3): 389–419.

Peckham, Irvine. 2009. "Online Placement in First-Year Writing." *College Composition and Communication* 60 (3): 517–40.

Perigo, Donald J., and M. Lee Upcraft. 1989. "Orientation Programs." In *The Freshman Year Experience: Helping Students Survive and Succeed in College,* ed. M. Lee Upcraft and John Gardner, 82–94. San Francisco: Jossey-Bass.

Ribble, Marcia. 2002. "Directed Self-Placement: The Shift from Placement to Pedagogy." PhD dissertation, Michigan State University, East Lansing.

Roberge, Mark. 2009. "A Teacher's Perspective on Generation 1.5." In *Generation 1.5 in College Composition: Teaching Academic Writing to U.S.-Educated Learners of ESL,* ed. Mark Roberge, Meryl Siegal, and Linda Harklau, 3–24. New York: Routledge.

Royer, Daniel J., and Roger Gilles. 1998. "Directed Self-Placement: An Attitude of Orientation." *College Composition and Communication* 50 (1): 54–70. http://dx.doi .org/10.2307/358352.

Royer, Daniel J., and Roger Gilles. 2003. "The Pragmatist Foundations of Directed Self-Placement." In *Directed Self-Placement: Principles and Practices,* ed. Daniel J. Royer and Roger Gilles, 49–71. Cresskill, NJ: Hampton Press.

Ruecker, Todd. 2011. "Improving the Placement of L2 Writers: The Students' Perspective." *WPA: Writing Program Administration* 35 (1): 91–117.

Saunders, Pearl. 2000. *Meeting the Needs of Entering Students through Appropriate Placement in Entry-Level Writing Courses.* Saint Louis, MO: Saint Louis Community College at Forest Park. Retrieved from ERIC database (ED 447505).

Schendel, Ellen, and Peggy O'Neill. 1999. "Exploring the Theories and Consequences of Self-Assessment through Ethical Inquiry." *Assessing Writing* 6 (2): 199–227. http://dx.doi.org/10.1016/S1075-2935(00)00008-8.

Seidman, Irving. 2006. *Interviewing as Qualitative Research: A Guide for Researchers in Education and Social Sciences.* New York: Teachers College, Columbia University.

Shuck, Gail. 2006. "Combating Monolingualism: A Novice Administrator's Challenge." *WPA: Writing Program Administration* 30 (1/2): 59–82.

Silva, Tony. 1994. "An Examination of Writing Program Administrators' Options of the Placement of ESL Students in First-Year Writing Classes." *WPA: Writing Program Administration* 18 (1/2): 37–43.

Strong-Krause, Diane. 2000. "Exploring the Effectiveness of Self-Assessment Strategies in ESL Placement." In *Learner-Directed Assessment in ESL*, ed. Glayol Ekbatani and Herbert Pierson, 49–74. Mahwah, NJ: Lawrence Erlbaum Associates.

Sullivan, Patrick, and David Nielsen. 2009. "Is a Writing Sample Necessary for 'Accurate Placement'?" *Journal of Developmental Education* 33 (2): 2–11.

Turnbull, Nick. 2004. "Rhetorical Agency as a Property of Questioning." *Philosophy & Rhetoric* 37 (3): 207–22. http://dx.doi.org/10.1353/par.2004.0024.

van Lier, Leo. 2009. "Forward: Agency, Self and Identity in Language Learning." In *Language Learner Autonomy: Policy, Curriculum, Classroom*, ed. Breffni O'Rourke and Lorna Carson, ix–xviii. New York: Peter Lang.

White, Edward M. 1994. *Teaching and Assessing Writing*. San Francisco: Jossey-Bass.

White, Eric R. 2000. "Developing Mission, Goals, and Objectives for the Advising Program." In *Academic Advising: A Comprehensive Handbook*, ed. Virginia Gordon and Wesley Habley, 180–91. San Francisco: Jossey-Bass Inc.

Williams, Jessica. 1995. "ESL Composition Program Administration in the United States." *Journal of Second Language Writing* 4 (2): 157–79. http://dx.doi.org/10.1016/1060-3743(95)90005-5.

Yancey, Kathleen. 1992. *Portfolios in the Writing Classroom: An Introduction*. Urbana: National Council of Teachers of English.

Young, Amanda. 2008. "Disciplinary Rhetorics, Rhetorical Agency, and the Construction of Voice." In *Rhetoric in Detail: Discourse Analyses of Rhetorical Talk and Text*, ed. Barbara Johnstone and Christopher Eisenhart, 227–46. Philadelphia: John Benjamins. http://dx.doi.org/10.1075/dapsac.31.14you.

ABOUT THE AUTHOR

Tanita Saenkhum is an assistant professor of English at the University of Tennessee, Knoxville, where she directs the English as a Second Language (ESL) program and teaches courses on second language writing and TESOL. She has published in *Journal of Second Language Writing*, *WPA: Writing Program Administration*, *Journal of English for Academic Purposes*, and *WPA-CompPile Research Bibliographies*. Her book chapters have appeared in different edited collections.

INDEX

academic advising, 77–78, 116; process of, 82–87; student evaluation of, 87–90
academic advisors, 18, 24, 27, 128; communication with, 120–21; consultation with, 42, 44, 47–48, 58–59; interviews with, 132–33; and multilingual students, 78–80; recommendations by, 11, 30–32, 37, 105; recommendations for, 113–14; role of, 81–82
accents, and class placement, 79, 105–6
acceptance, of placement, 41–42
Accuplacer Test, 18, 42– 43, 45–46, 51, 84–85, 90, 105; and self-placement, 54, 55–56
ACT scores, 80; placement using, 18, 35–36, 86, 88, 105
administrators. *See* writing program administrators
advisors. *See* academic advisors
Afia, 22, 26–27, 33, 52; class evaluation by, 45–47, 105–6; class experience of, 43–44; placement negotiation by, 40–41, 42–43, 50, 51; registration decisions of, 44–45
agency, 6, 37, 65; acts of, 26–27; definitions of, 9–11; emerging conditions for, 109–10; in placement decisions, 50–51, 74, 107–16. *See also* student agency
Ahearn, Laura, 9
Ana, 22–23, 35–36, 39(n4), 89, 106; placement information, 112–13
Anderson, Perry, 9
Anne, 25, 93, 94, 96, 99
anthropology, agency in, 9, 37
Askar, 23, 32, 88

assessment, direct and indirect, 7, 12, 13
ASU, 5; communication at, 113; research at, 20–21; writing program at, 17–20, 117–18

Beverly, 25, 93, 96, 99; on placement issues, 95, 97
bilingualism, 35
breakout sessions, 121
brochure, placement, 118, 119(fig.)

Campbell, Karlyn, 10
CBT. *See* computer-based test
Chan, 22, 27, 31, 32, 36, 64, 87; decision making by, 72–73, 76, 109–10; on ENG 107, 66–67
choice, 10, 11
class discussion, as challenge, 93–94
coding, 137; reliability of, 138–40; tables, 141–43
College of Liberal Arts and Sciences' Office of Student and Academic Programs, 120
communication: with academic advisors, 120–21; improving, 112, 113; with writing teachers, 98–99, 102–3, 106–7
computer-based test (CBT), 125
courses, 17, 87; academic advising on, 77–78; descriptions of, 124–26; knowledge of, 51–52; titles of, 97–98
Crusan, Deborah, 13
cultural diversity, and academic advising, 78
curriculum design: for differing abilities, 62–63; L2, 53–54

Dan, 25, 95, 96